LIVE LIFE BIG

Don't LEAVE Your DREAM, LIVE Your DREAM!

Copyright © 2024 Michael Koku

All rights reserved. No part of this publication may be reproduced, distributed, or transmitted in any form or by any means, including photocopying, recording, or other electronic or mechanical methods, without the prior written permission of the publisher, except in the case of brief quotations embodied in critical reviews and certain other noncommercial uses permitted by copyright law.

Paperback ISBN: 979-8-9888845-6-9

Published by ROYAL ENVOYS INC.

TABLE OF CONTENTS

Dedication 1

Appreciation 3

Introduction: Are You Leaving Or Living Your Dream? 5

Chapter One: Are You Living Your Dream Or Someone Else's? 9

Chapter Two: Living Life Big: The Power Of Living Your Own Dream! 23

Chapter Three: Don't Leave Your Dream, Live Your Dream! 45

Chapter Four: It Is Never Too Late To Live Your Dream! 57

Chapter Five: Your Dream Is Not About You—It's About Others! 65

Chapter Six: Practical Blueprint For Living Life Big! 79

Chapter Seven: Dream Factor 89

Chapter Eight: Resilience Factor 95

Chapter Nine: Embrace Teamwork Factor 103

Chapter Ten: Accountability Partnership Factor: Your Bridge From Intention To Reality 111

Chapter Eleven: Mentorship Factor: Accelerating Your Journey 117

Epilogue: Live Life Big—Your Dream Awaits You!.......129

Meet The Author 135

Esperanza Manifold Concepts Llc 137

Lamp Global Community 139

DEDICATION

"Live for yourself and you live in vain. Live for others and you will live again." —Robert Nesta Marley.

This book is dedicated to two of my greatest mentors, whose lives embody the essence of living for others and leaving a legacy that transcends time:

Dr. Myles Munroe

A visionary leader, philosopher, pastor, and teacher, Dr. Myles Munroe founded Bahamas Faith Ministries International and Myles Munroe International. His wisdom and passion for empowering people globally made him a beacon of hope and transformation. As CEO and Chairman of the International Third World Leaders Association and President of the International Leadership Training Institute, he devoted his life to unlocking the potential of others. His legacy continues to inspire millions long after his passing a decade ago.

Dr. David Oyedepo

A man of unwavering faith and purpose, Dr. David Oyedepo is the founder of Living Faith Church Worldwide and Presiding Bishop of Faith Tabernacle in Ota, Nigeria. As Chancellor of Covenant University and Landmark University, he has nurtured generations of leaders, teaching them that true success is measured by the impact you make on others. His teachings have transformed lives, and his life's work serves as a powerful example of what it means to LIVE LIFE BIG.

To these remarkable giants, thank you for teaching us that LIVING LIFE BIG is not about fame or fortune but about making a meaningful difference in the lives of others. Your influence will forever be remembered.

APPRECIATION

Creating this life-changing book has been a journey filled with dedication, sacrifice, and collaboration. I am deeply grateful to the following exceptional individuals who contributed their time, expertise, and heart to this project:

David Tolu Oridota: Thank you for graciously allowing me to share your inspiring story within these pages. Your journey is a beacon of hope and a testament to what it means to LIVE LIFE BIG.

Adewole Sosanya and Dr. Oludare Osiboye: To my incomparable editors, your meticulous attention to detail and unwavering commitment to excellence elevated this book to new heights. Your insights were invaluable.

Temitope Adewale: My compassionate publisher, thank you for your relentless dedication in bringing this vision to life. Your belief in this project was a source of strength.

The TLC Personalities: To the 21 dynamic and effective leaders of the LAMP Global Community, thank you for collaborating with me on our shared mission of global transformation. Together, we are not just living life—we're LIVING LIFE BIG. Your leadership and partnership are invaluable.

Adebola Koku (MCQ): My Charming Queen, your constant support, encouragement, and love throughout this process have been the wind beneath my wings. You walked this journey with me, and for that, I am eternally grateful.

To each of you, thank you for your sacrifice, your input, and your unwavering belief in this book. Indeed, it takes a crew to make a brew—and together, we've created something truly special.

INTRODUCTION: ARE YOU LEAVING OR LIVING YOUR DREAM?

"Believe in your dreams, no matter how impossible they seem." — Walt Disney.

David Joseph Schwartz, Jr. (March 23, 1927 – December 6, 1987), an American motivational writer and coach, is best known for his transformative book, The Magic of Thinking Big (1959). As a professor of marketing and Chair of Consumer Finance at Georgia State University, Schwartz dedicated his life to teaching others the power of belief and the importance of living one's dreams.

In his best-selling book, "The Magic of Thinking Big" Schwartz shares a poignant and timeless story. It's about a young writer, brimming with passion and dreams of a career in journalism. However, he abandoned his dream, swayed by the notion that journalism wouldn't pay well. He chose a different field with higher pay and seemingly greater incentives. Years later, despite financial success, he was filled with regret. His job, while lucrative, lacked the fulfillment and joy that journalism could have brought. This story underscores a vital truth: living your dream is the only guarantee for a life of true significance and genuine fulfillment.

Today, many people find themselves in similar situations—pursuing careers driven by external rewards rather than internal passions and eternal rewards. They leave their dreams behind and end up in a cycle of dissatisfaction and disinterest, merely existing rather than truly living.

As Schwartz aptly put it, "Believe it can be done. When you believe something can be done, really believe, your mind will find the way to do it. Believing a solution paves the way to solution." Living your dream requires belief and courage, but the rewards are immeasurable.

Oprah Winfrey, a living testament to the power of pursuing one's dreams, once said, "The biggest adventure you can take is to live the life of your dreams." This sentiment echoes Schwartz's teachings and highlights the fulfillment that comes from aligning your life with your passions.

Steve Jobs, co-founder of Apple Inc., also emphasized the importance of following one's dreams: "Your work is going to fill a large part of your life, and the only way to be truly satisfied is to do what you believe is great work. And the only way to do great work is to love what you do." Jobs' words resonate deeply with Schwartz's philosophy, reinforcing the idea that true success and happiness stem from pursuing what you love.

Living your dream is not without challenges. It requires perseverance, resilience, and an unwavering belief in your vision. But the journey, as Schwartz and countless others have shown, is worth it. The sense of fulfillment, purpose, and joy that comes from living your dream far outweighs the temporary comforts of a well-paying but unfulfilling job.

Living your dream is the only path to a life of true significance and genuine fulfillment. As Schwartz said,

"Think big and you'll live big. You'll live big in happiness. You'll live big in accomplishment. Big in income. Big in friends. Big in respect." Embrace your dreams, believe in them, and watch as your life transforms in ways you never imagined.

CHAPTER ONE
ARE YOU LIVING YOUR DREAM OR SOMEONE ELSE'S?

"You only have one life to live. Make sure it's yours."
– Eleanor Brownn.

Imagine reaching the end of your life and looking back with a heart full of regret. This stark reality was uncovered by Bronnie Ware, a palliative care nurse who spent years caring for patients in their final days. Ware's profound observations, shared in her book *The Top Five Regrets of the Dying*, reveal the most common regrets expressed by those nearing the end of their journey:

1. **I wish I'd had the courage to live a life true to myself, not the life others expected of me.**
2. **I wish I hadn't worked so hard.**
3. **I wish I'd had the courage to express my feelings.**
4. **I wish I had stayed in touch with my friends.**
5. **I wish that I had let myself be happier.**

The Pain of Unrealized Dreams

These poignant regrets, shared originally in a 2009 blog post by Ware, resonated globally and were later expanded into a memoir in 2012 translated into 27 languages. A 2018 study echoed Ware's findings, emphasizing that many people regret not pursuing their dreams and failing to reach their full potential.

[https://en.wikipedia.org/wiki/The_Top_Five_Regrets_of_the_Dying. Accessed August 7, 2024].

Societal Expectations vs. Personal Fulfillment

Many find themselves ensnared in careers shaped by societal expectations or financial pressures, only to realize too late that they are living someone else's dream. This disheartening truth highlights the crucial need to follow your passions and aspirations.

The Magic of Thinking Big

David Schwartz, Jr., in his timeless book *The Magic of Thinking Big*, asserts that true fulfillment comes from living your own dream. He challenges us to avoid settling for mere existence and instead to embrace a life of significance and joy. Living your own dream means breaking free from the chains of societal norms and financial constraints to pursue what truly makes your heart sing.

The Courage to Live True to Yourself

The number one regret, "I wish I'd had the courage to live a life true to myself, not the life others expected of me," highlights a universal truth. To live a life true to ourselves, we must dare to LIVE our dreams instead of LEAVING them by choosing the life others expect of us.

From Medicine to Leadership – My Personal Journey

I am a living example of someone who dared to LIVE their dreams. Nineteen years ago, I completed my medical training in West African largest city premier university and practiced as a physician for three years. Then, my life took a dramatic turn. After immigrating to the United States with my newly wedded wife, I announced to my siblings that I would not be practicing as a physician anymore but would instead pursue and live my dreams.

Stepping Towards Destiny

It seemed like a suicidal decision, leaving the security of a stable career for the uncertainty of the unknown. Author and leadership expert Craig Groeschel aptly said, "To step towards your destiny, you have to step away from your security." That is exactly what I did.

Building a New Path

We settled in Raleigh, North Carolina for three months before moving to Philadelphia, Pennsylvania. There, I worked with the Salvation Army Greater Philadelphia Area for ten years and was awarded the 2018 Employee Award for Meritorious Service to Humanity and the Community. In 2020, I left the organization and launched my own leadership development and coaching company, Esperanza Manifold Concepts LLC as a Maxwell Leadership Team Independent Executive Director, Speaker, Coach, and Trainer.

Creating a Global Impact

Since then, I have published seven new books between August 2023 to August 2024 [excluding my first two books published when I was in medical school in year 2000 and 2003] and realized my dream of global transformation by founding a global leadership development community, LAMP Global Community last year. We have grown to twenty-one dedicated leaders with shared values, purpose and a positive attitude to change the world for the good. Together, we have hosted leadership global masterclasses and five virtual global conferences, impacting lives worldwide. Our sixth virtual global conference, Parents Empowered Annual Global Conference 2.0 is coming up on Saturday, December 21, 2024, and the seventh virtual global conference, Made For More Global Leadership Conference 4.0, is scheduled for Saturday, March 1, 2025.

A Resonating Truth

The American poet and advocate of the abolition of slavery in the United States, John Greenleaf Whittier, once said, "For all sad words of tongue or pen, the saddest are these: 'It might have been.'" This profound statement resonates deeply with me. I refuse to end my days with the regret of not having the courage to live a life true to myself by living my dream and LIVING LIFE BIG!

Embrace Your True Self – There is Only One You in the Universe!

As I reflect on my journey, I urge you to embrace your true self and live your dreams. Don't let fear or societal expectations dictate your path. Live authentically, pursue your passions, and strive for a life of significance and joy. Remember, you only have one life to live—make sure it's yours. At the end of your life, you will have no other person to blame but yourself for leaving your dream instead of living your dream by having the courage to be true to yourself and not the life that others expected of you!

Discover the Fulfillment of Following Your True Passion!

David Meltzer, a speaker, author, and entrepreneur, wisely said, "Just because somebody loves you doesn't mean they give you good advice." This sentiment rings true in the story of an American billionaire businessman and investor, Michael Dell. He is the founder, chairman, and CEO of Dell Technologies, one of the world's largest technology infrastructure companies.

Michael Dell is a man who dared to pursue his passion despite well-meaning but misguided advice. Michael Dell's journey from a tech-obsessed teenager to the founder of one of the world's largest technology companies serves as a powerful example of the importance of living one's dream instead of someone else's dream.

The Early Years: A Tech Prodigy in the Making

Michael Dell was born on February 23, 1965, in Houston, Texas. From an early age, Dell exhibited a fascination with technology and business. By the time he was in his early teens, he had already shown an entrepreneurial spirit. At 15, Dell purchased his first computer, an Apple II, and promptly disassembled it to understand its inner workings. This hands-on experience ignited a passion that would shape his future.

Despite his evident interest in technology, Dell's parents envisioned a different path for him. They encouraged him to pursue a career in medicine, believing it would offer stability and success. In deference to their wishes, Dell enrolled at the University of Texas at Austin as a pre-med student. However, his heart was not in it.

Discovering the Dream: From Hobby to Obsession

Michael Dell's fascination with technology began in his teenage years. While his peers were engrossed in typical high school activities, Michael spent his time disassembling and rebuilding computers. This hobby wasn't just a pastime; it was the spark of a dream.

"Passion is what drives me. I am passionate about computers and technology," Dell has often said.

Defying Expectations: Choosing Technology Over Medicine

Michael's parents had high hopes for him to become a doctor. However, the compelling pull of his dream was too strong to ignore. As a freshman in college, while he was supposed to be preparing for a medical career, Michael spent his time buying computer parts at wholesale prices and assembling custom machines for professionals like lawyers and doctors for their office use.

Following the Dream: From Dorm Room to Boardroom

Michael Dell's entrepreneurial instincts couldn't be suppressed. In his dorm room, he started a business upgrading personal computers, focusing on selling directly to customers. His enterprise grew rapidly, and within a short period, Dell realized that his true calling lay not in medicine, but in revolutionizing the computer industry.

Against his parents' wishes, Dell dropped out of college after just one year to fully commit to his thriving business. This bold decision marked the beginning of what would become Dell Technologies, a multinational corporation that changed the way computers were sold and built.

Dell once remarked, "You don't have to be a genius or a visionary, or even a college graduate for that matter, to be successful. You just need a framework and a dream,"

The Birth of a Business Empire

In 1984, with just $1,000 in startup capital, Michael Dell founded Dell Computer Corporation. His direct-to-consumer model, which eliminated the middleman and allowed for customized orders, set Dell apart from its competitors. This innovative approach quickly gained traction, and by the early 1990s, Dell Computer Corporation was a major player in the industry.

Dell's commitment to his dream and his innovative business strategies paid off. Today, Dell Technologies is a global leader in technology, providing products and services to customers in over 180 countries. Michael Dell's net worth is estimated to be $124 billion as of March 2024 according to the Bloomberg Billionaires Index, making him the 10th richest person in the world.

Throughout his journey, Michael Dell has been guided by a vision and determination to follow his passion. His story is a testament to the power of living one's dream.

LEAVING Your DREAM: The Path Not Taken

Had Michael Dell adhered to his parents' expectations, he might have become a doctor—a respectable profession, but one that wasn't his dream. This path would have meant leaving his true passion behind, potentially leading to a life of unfulfilled potential and what-ifs.

"Real entrepreneurs have what I call the three P's: passion, persistence, and problem-solving," Dell explained.

LIVING Your DREAM: The Path Worth Taking

Michael Dell chose to live his dream. His story is a testament to the power of following one's passion, despite societal and familial pressures. Dell's journey from a curious teenager to a tech industry titan underscores the profound impact of living your dream.

"Don't be trapped by dogma—which is living with the results of other people's thinking," he emphasizes.

LIVING vs. LEAVING Your DREAM: The Ultimate Question

Michael Dell's story vividly illustrates the difference between living and leaving your dream. Had he followed the conventional path laid out by his parents, the world might have missed out on one of its greatest innovators. Instead, Dell chose to live his dream, transforming not only his own life but also the global technology landscape.

Living your dream means pursuing your passion with unwavering commitment, regardless of the obstacles or the opinions of others. It's about finding fulfillment and significance in your work, leading to a life of true meaning. Leaving your dream, on the other hand, often results in a life filled with regret, boredom, and unfulfilled potential. My mentor, Dr. John Maxwell said, "Commitment is not an event. It is a process. Anytime you make a commitment to something, it will be tested."

The big question is: Are you leaving or living your dreams? It is only by living your dreams that you can unlock your full potential and become a blessing to humanity. When we live our dreams, we give others permission to live their own dreams which will result in making this world a better place. When we leave our dreams, the decision may be private, but the consequences are never private because others will not have someone to model their lives after.

LEAVING or LIVING Your DREAM is Your Choice

Michael Dell's inspiring journey challenges us to reflect on our own lives. Are you leaving your dreams behind, constrained by expectations and fears? Or are you boldly living your dreams, driven by passion and purpose?

In the words of Michael Dell, "It's through curiosity and looking at opportunities in new ways that we've always mapped our path." Your dream is your unique map to navigate an extraordinary life. The choice between LEAVING and LIVING your dream is yours to make. It's the difference between settling for mediocrity and striving for milestone accomplishments. It's about choosing significance over safety, passion over predictability.

Remember, every invention you see started as a dream. You have the power to bring your dreams to life. As Henry David Thoreau said, "Go confidently in the direction of your dreams. Live the life you have imagined." Dare to be a producer. Dare to live your dream. Don't live as an imitation which brings limitation to the full expression of your infinite potential; dare to live as an original!

Dare to Live Your Dream and Not Someone Else's!

"Whatever you think, be sure that it is what you want; whatever you feel, be sure that it is what you feel." These words by T.S. Eliot, one of the greatest poets of the 20th century, carry profound wisdom. They remind us to introspect and ensure that our dreams and aspirations are truly our own.

The Burden of Borrowed Dreams

Have you ever felt burdened by a path that seems more exhausting than exhilarating? This often happens when we chase dreams that aren't genuinely ours. Borrowed dreams, no matter how grand, lack the conviction, passion, and dedication required to bring them to fruition. Without a personal connection, these dreams become a heavy burden, weighing down our spirits and sapping our energy.

Conversely, living your dream infuses life with purpose, energy, and joy. When you pursue what genuinely ignites your passion, every step forward becomes a celebration. Your dream, born from your deepest desires and values, fuels your determination and perseverance. Life becomes not just a series of tasks, but a meaningful journey filled with fulfilling adventures and rewarding outcomes.

The Consequences of Living Someone Else's Dream

Living someone else's dream is essentially abandoning your own. This can lead to a life of dissatisfaction and regret. Imagine climbing a ladder only to get to the top and realize it's leaning against the wrong wall. Each step you take away from your true passion creates a gap that can only be filled by rediscovering and pursuing what truly matters to you.

Crafting Your Unique Path

Living your dream isn't just about professional success; it's about personal fulfillment. It's about finding joy in the journey and embracing your passions wholeheartedly.

Here are some steps to help you live a life true to yourself:

1. Reflect on Your True Desires

Take time to introspect and identify what you genuinely want out of life. What are your passions? What brings you joy?

2. Set Authentic Goals

Once you know what you want, set realistic and authentic goals that align with your passions and aspirations.

3. Take Bold Steps

Don't be afraid to take risks and make changes. It's never too late to start living your dream.

4. Seek Support and Mentorship

Surround yourself with supportive individuals who encourage and inspire you to pursue your dreams.

5. Embrace Happiness

Allow yourself to be happy and content with the life you choose. Celebrate your achievements and learn from your setbacks.

Embrace Your True Self

Remember, you only have one life to live—make sure it's yours. Don't let the fear of societal expectations or financial pressures dictate your path. Embrace your dreams, live with passion, and strive for a life of true significance and joy.

Self-Activity for Chapter One

Reflect on the following powerful questions to help you determine if you're living your own dream or someone else's:

1. Self-Awareness:

- Are you genuinely passionate about the life you're currently living? If not, what parts feel forced or unaligned with who you truly are?
- What excites you and fills you with energy? Compare that with what you do day-to-day. Are you investing time in your true passions?

2. Societal and External Expectations:

- How much of your current life is shaped by societal norms or the expectations of others (family, friends, colleagues)?

- When you make decisions, do you prioritize what feels right to you or what will gain approval from others?

3. **Regret Avoidance:**

    - Imagine yourself at the end of your life, looking back. What would your biggest regret be if you continue on your current path? Are you at risk of saying, "I wish I'd had the courage to live a life true to myself, not the life others expected of me?"

    - What steps can you take today to reduce or eliminate the possibility of such a regret?

4. **Fear and Courage:**

    - What fears are holding you back from fully pursuing your dream? Are they rooted in fear of failure, judgment, or financial insecurity?

    - How can you start building the courage to take small steps toward living your dream, even if it means stepping away from security?

5. **Personal Fulfillment:**

    - What would living a life true to yourself look like? Picture your ideal life, free from external pressures—how different is it from your current reality?

    - What areas of your life bring you true fulfillment and joy? How can you expand those areas to occupy more space in your life?

6. Purpose and Passion:

- Have you taken the time to define what your personal dream looks like, or are you still following someone else's version of success?
- What would you do with your time and talents if you didn't have to worry about anyone else's opinions or expectations?

7. Legacy:

- How would you like to be remembered at the end of your life? Are you working toward that legacy now, or do you need to make changes to align with it?

Action Steps:

- Write down your personal definition of success. Is it based on your own desires or influenced by what others expect of you?
- Create a small, actionable goal that moves you closer to living your dream—no matter how minor it seems—and commit to achieving it this week.

Remember, the first step to living your dream is recognizing where you're not being true to yourself and having the courage to make necessary changes. As Michael Dell once said, "Your dream is your unique map to an extraordinary life."

Note: *"The best effect of any book is that it excites the reader to self-activity."* – Thomas Carlyle.

CHAPTER TWO
LIVING LIFE BIG: THE POWER OF LIVING YOUR OWN DREAM!

"97% of the people who quit too soon are employed by the 3% who never gave up on their dreams."
– Elon Musk.

Stop Settling for Small—You Were Made for More!

Michelangelo once said, *"The greater danger for most of us lies not in setting our aim too high and falling short, but in setting our aim too low and achieving our mark."* This profound truth speaks to the core of why so many settle for average, for living life small. Too often, people fail to realize that they were *made for more*. The danger of limiting oneself to mediocrity is far more devastating than the risks of reaching for greatness and momentarily stumbling.

We live in a world where it's easy to get comfortable, aiming just low enough to avoid discomfort but missing incredible opportunities beyond that mark. **LAMP GLOBAL COMMUNITY**, which I am privileged to lead in collaboration with **twenty-one dynamic leaders and dedicated allies**, is on a mission to awaken hearts and minds to the truth that **you have the right to live life big**. Our virtual **MADE FOR MORE GLOBAL LEADERSHIP CONFERENCE** exists to shatter those limits and inspire individuals worldwide to quit thinking average and start living life with compelling purpose and propelling passion.

MADE FOR MORE—And We Mean It!

On **September 7, 2024**, we hosted the **MADE FOR MORE GLOBAL LEADERSHIP CONFERENCE 3.0**, and we didn't just talk about growth—we witnessed it. With more than **500 registrants from all over the world**, we saw instant testimonials of lives transformations, dreams reignited, and potentials unlocked and about to be unleashed. Each speaker brought a fresh fire, a burning reminder that **average is the enemy of greatness**.

We didn't stop there! To further encourage and appreciate our attendees, eight of the participants won $50 Amazon gift cards or cash equivalents. The joy and gratitude we received in return made every moment of the conference worth it.

Here's a heartfelt message from one of our attendees, **Oluwapelumi Osunlola**, who was also a prize winner after she received the alert for her $50 gift in her bank account:

"Overwhelmed with Gratitude!"

Alert Received!

"I'm overwhelmed with gratitude and joy as I write this note to express my heartfelt thanks for the incredible gift you've given me. Your generosity and thoughtfulness have truly touched my heart.

This gift is more than just a present—it's a reminder of your love, care, and kindness to humanity and the world. This gift means a lot to me, and with the deepest thanks and appreciation from my heart, I say God bless the entire organizers of the *Made for More* conference.

You're the best! Can't wait for the next conference."

YOU TOO CAN LIVE LIFE BIG

Oluwapelumi's experience is a testament to the power of aiming higher and embracing the belief that we are *Made for More*. Whether through inspiring keynotes, practical leadership tools, or life-changing stories, this conference equips people to step into greatness.

"You are never too old to set another goal or to dream a new dream." — C.S. Lewis.

The question is:

Will you continue to settle for less, or will you seize the opportunity to aim high, live boldly, and create the life you were truly meant to live? At *Made For More*, we believe you're destined for greatness. Don't wait for life to happen to you—take charge, dream big, and live life with purpose!

We can't wait to see you at the next MADE FOR MORE GLOBAL LEADERSHIP CONFERENCE 4.0 next March 1, 2025—where even more dreams will be set ablaze, and more lives will be transformed! The conference is virtual, and you can attend from anywhere in the world with a good internet connection. Registration is now open, and you can register now at lgcleadeship.com/will. General admission is free. VIP admission with more benefits is $47.

Challenging Mediocrity

As **Dr. John C. Maxwell** wisely put it: *"Small thinking limits our potential, while big thinking expands it."* Those who attended the conference were challenged to expand their thinking, to push beyond the ordinary, and to embrace the *extraordinary* within. Too many people are sleepwalking through life, unaware that there's a vast potential inside of them just waiting to be unleashed.

Dream Big—Live Life Big!

Another inspiring quote comes from **Les Brown**, who reminds us: *"Shoot for the moon. Even if you miss, you'll land among the stars."* We firmly believe in this mindset. To **live life big**, you must first *think big*. The conference was a call to action—an invitation to stop shrinking your dreams to fit your fears and start growing your dreams to match your faith and potential.

More Testimonies of Impact

Many attendees from the Made For More Global Leadership Conference 3.0 also shared instant testimonials of how their perspective shifted dramatically. They left the conference no longer satisfied with small ambitions but instead empowered to pursue **life-changing goals**.

Your Potential Is Waiting—Are You Ready?

"Don't live the same year 75 times and call it a life," said **Robin Sharma**. If you've ever felt that there's more to life than the daily grind, that you're capable of achieving something far greater than you've allowed yourself to believe, you're right. The time to **live life big** is now.

Our goal through the **MADE FOR MORE GLOBAL LEADERSHIP CONFERENCE** is to help you break through those mental barriers and see yourself as the remarkable, capable, and gifted person you truly are. **Stop settling for small, because you are made for more!**

Rise to the Challenge—Take the Leap!

In the words of **Steve Jobs**, *"The people who are crazy enough to think they can change the world are the ones who do."* It's time to get a little crazy with your dreams, a little wild with your vision, and a lot relentless in your pursuit of greatness. Don't wait for permission. **You are worthy of a life beyond imagined limits.**

As **LAMP GLOBAL COMMUNITY**, we are committed to creating these environments where you're not just encouraged but *challenged* to dream bigger and reach higher. You are made for more—and we're here to remind you of that truth, time and time again.

Your Life, Your Dream, Your Time!

Are you ready to take the next step? **Your dream is not too big—it's exactly what you need to become the person you were always meant to be.** Let's go from thinking average to thinking *exceptional*. It's time to unleash your potential, live your dream, and live life big!

Remember:

"You don't have to be great to start, but you have to start to be great."—**Zig Ziglar.**

This is your moment. This is your opportunity. **The world is waiting for the greatness only you can bring. Quit thinking average. Aim high and LIVE LIFE BIG!**

IT'S A DREAMER'S WORLD!

"Every great dream begins with a dreamer." – Harriet Tubman.

Elon Reeve Musk, born June 28, 1971, is a name synonymous with innovation and relentless pursuit of dreams. As the wealthiest man in the world in July 2024, with a net worth estimated at US$235.4 billion by Forbes, Musk's journey is a testament to what happens when you refuse to give up on your dreams.

From Pretoria to the Stars

Musk's story begins in Pretoria, South Africa, where he was born to model Maye and businessman and engineer Errol Musk. His early life was marked by curiosity and ambition. At 18, Musk moved to Canada, acquiring citizenship through his Canadian-born mother, and enrolled at Queen's University in Kingston. After two years, he transferred to the University of Pennsylvania, earning Bachelor's degrees in Economics and Physics. His quest for knowledge and innovation led him to California in 1995, where he briefly attended Stanford University before deciding to drop out after just two days.

The Birth of Zip2 and PayPal

With his brother Kimbal, Musk co-founded Zip2, an online city guide software company. Zip2 was acquired by Compaq in 1999 for $307 million, marking Musk's first major entrepreneurial success. That same year, he co-founded X.com, an online bank that later became PayPal after merging with Confinity. When eBay acquired PayPal for $1.5 billion in 2002, Musk was just getting started.

SpaceX and Tesla: Dreaming Beyond the Sky

Using $100 million from the sale of PayPal, Musk founded SpaceX in 2002, aiming to revolutionize space travel. His vision for a multi-planetary existence pushed the boundaries of what was possible. In 2004, Musk invested in Tesla Motors, Inc., becoming its chairman and later the CEO and product architect. Tesla's electric vehicles have since transformed the automotive industry, championing sustainable energy and innovation.

Expanding Horizons: SolarCity, Neuralink, and Beyond

Musk's ventures didn't stop there. In 2006, he helped create SolarCity, which later merged with Tesla to become Tesla Energy. His 2013 proposal for the hyperloop, a high-speed vactrain system, showcased his futuristic thinking. Co-founding OpenAI in 2015 and Neuralink in 2016, Musk continued to push the envelope, exploring artificial intelligence and brain-computer interfaces.

The Boring Company and X Corp.

In 2016, Musk founded The Boring Company to revolutionize tunnel construction. His 2022 acquisition of Twitter for $44 billion, which was later rebranded as X, illustrated his influence in the social media landscape. Most recently, in March 2023, Musk founded xAI, an artificial intelligence company aimed at developing advanced AI technologies.

Pursuit is the Proof of Desire

Elon Musk's journey is a powerful reminder of his own words: "97% of the people who quit too soon are employed by 3% who never gave up on their dreams." His story is a vivid illustration of the incredible impact of living life big and relentlessly pursuing your dreams.

American animation film producer, Walt Disney said, "All our dreams can come true, if we have the courage to pursue them." Courage to persevere on your dreams is a huge separator between winners and quitters. American media mogul, Oprah Winfrey once said, "The biggest adventure you can take is to live the life of your dreams." We cannot live life big when we abandon [leave] our own dreams and live someone else's dream. We need to heed the words of the great poet, Henry David Thoreau who said, "Go confidently in the direction of your dreams. Live the life you have imagined."

Elon Musk's life is a beacon of inspiration, proving that with perseverance, innovation, and an unwavering belief in one's dreams, anything is possible. His story, combined with the wisdom of other great leaders, serves as a powerful call to action: to live life big and never give up on your dreams.

Success Redefined!

"Real success is knowing your purpose in life, growing to your maximum potential, and sowing seeds that benefits others." – John Maxwell.

Danny Thomas once said, "Success in life has nothing to do with what you gain in life or accomplish for yourself. It's what you do for others." In this profound statement, Thomas redefines success, shifting the focus from personal achievements to the impact one has on the lives of others. He emphasized significance—the act of sowing seeds that benefit others. As eloquently put by John Maxwell: "The key to significance is sowing seeds that benefit others." This philosophy not only guided Thomas's life but also inspired his monumental contributions to society.

A Dream That Saved Lives: The Birth of St. Jude Children's Research Hospital

Danny Thomas embodied the spirit of living life big by transforming his dreams into reality. Born Amos Muzyad Yaqoob Kairouz on January 6, 1912, in Deerfield, Michigan, Thomas was one of ten children in a Maronite Catholic immigrant family from Bsharri, Lebanon. Despite the challenges he faced as a starving actor, Thomas harbored a dream of making a significant difference in the world. His vision materialized in the form of St. Jude Children's Research Hospital in Memphis, Tennessee.

With the support of Dr. Lemuel Diggs and close friend Anthony Abraham, an auto magnate in Miami, Florida, Thomas founded the hospital in 1962. Driven by his fervent belief that "No child should die in the dawn of life," Thomas dedicated himself to raising funds for the hospital. Today, St. Jude stands as a leading center in pediatric medicine, particularly in the fight against pediatric cancer.

A Legacy of Hope and Healing

St. Jude Children's Research Hospital has not only treated children from all 50 states and around the world but also advanced medical research and treatment protocols. In 1996, Dr. Peter C. Doherty from St. Jude's Immunology Department was co-awarded the Nobel Prize in Physiology or Medicine for groundbreaking discoveries on how the immune system combats virus-infected cells.

Under Thomas's vision and leadership, St. Jude expanded to include eight affiliate hospitals across the United States. As a 501(c)(3) nonprofit organization, it operates with an annual budget of over $1.4 billion, funded by nearly $1.5 billion in donations. This remarkable financial support underscores the global community's belief in Thomas's mission.

Global Impact: Collaborating for a Cure

St. Jude's impact extends far beyond its Memphis headquarters. Recognized by the World Health Organization as its first "Collaborating Center for Childhood Cancer," St. Jude is committed to improving survival rates for rare pediatric cancers from 20% to as much as 60% by 2030. This ambitious goal highlights the hospital's unwavering dedication to saving lives and advancing global health.

Live Your Dream Big, Live Life Big: The Power of Significance

Danny Thomas's journey from a struggling actor to the founder of a world-renowned research hospital exemplifies the profound impact of living a life of significance. By prioritizing the well-being of others, Thomas not only achieved his dreams but also left an enduring legacy that continues to inspire and save lives. His story serves as a powerful reminder that true success lies in the seeds we sow for the benefit of others, urging us all to dream big, live big, and strive for significance.

OTHER EXAMPLARY INDIVIDUALS WHO LIVED LIFE BIG BY LIVING THEIR DREAMS

"Life is an exciting business, and it is most exciting when lived for others." – Helen Keller.

Living a life of significance means going beyond mere existence. It's about dreaming big, achieving those dreams, and using your success to make a meaningful impact on others. True significance is found when we sow seeds that benefit others, creating a legacy that endures beyond our own achievements.

Hobby Lobby Founder, David Green: An Extraordinary Leader

David Green, the founder and CEO of Hobby Lobby, epitomizes the essence of living life big. From humble beginnings, Green's story is a testament to how living your dream with purpose and generosity can transform lives on a grand scale.

From $600 to an $8 Billion Empire

In 1972, David Green started Hobby Lobby with a mere $600 loan. What began as a small home-based business has grown into the world's largest privately-owned arts and crafts retailer, boasting nearly 1,000 stores and employing approximately 50,000 individuals nationwide. This remarkable journey from modest beginnings to an $8 billion empire is a testament to Green's entrepreneurial spirit and unwavering faith.

Prioritizing People Over Profits

"Business as usual is not an option for us. We have a different perspective—a higher purpose that extends beyond profits." - David Green

David Green's business philosophy places paramount importance on the well-being of his employees and customers. Guided by his Christian faith, Green has instituted policies that reflect his values, such as closing all Hobby Lobby stores on Sundays to allow employees to spend time with their families and faith communities.

A Heart for Giving

"It's not about how much we give, but how much love we put into giving." - Mother Teresa.

Green's commitment to philanthropy is as impressive as his business success. He has pledged half of Hobby Lobby's pretax earnings to evangelical ministries, with his lifetime giving estimated to be upwards of $500 million. His philanthropic efforts have supported numerous

Christian organizations, education, and humanitarian causes.

One notable example is the $20 million donation to Highlands College in Birmingham, Alabama. This generous gift fully funded the institution's first residence hall, which will house 252 students and support their development for full-time Christian ministry.

Legacy of Impact

"Success is not the key to happiness. Happiness is the key to success. If you love what you are doing, you will be successful." - Albert Schweitzer.

David Green's story is more than just a tale of business success; it's a powerful narrative of how living your dream with purpose and compassion can lead to a life of true significance. By prioritizing his employees' well-being, closing stores on Sundays, and dedicating substantial resources to charitable causes, Green has shown that a business can thrive while making profound impact on the world.

Living your dream and sowing seeds that benefit others is the key to a life of significance. David Green's journey from a $600 loan to a multi-billion-dollar enterprise is a shining example of living life big. His unwavering commitment to faith, family, and philanthropy serves as an inspiration for us all to pursue our dreams with passion and purpose, and to use our success to make a difference in the lives of others.

As you embark on your own journey, remember the words of David Green: "We are stewards of the lives and resources God has entrusted to us. It's not about how much we have, but how we use what we have to serve others."

Chick-fil-A Founder, Truett Cathy: A Visionary Leader

Truett Cathy, the founder of Chick-fil-A, exemplifies the spirit of living life big. From a modest start with a small loan, Cathy's journey is a powerful story of how living your dream with purpose and generosity can transform lives on a grand scale.

From $10,400 to a Billion-Dollar Brand

In 1946, Truett Cathy opened his first restaurant, the Dwarf Grill, in Hapeville, Georgia, with a $10,400 loan. His dedication to quality and customer service laid the foundation for Chick-fil-A, which would become one of the most successful fast-food chains in the world. Today, Chick-fil-A boasts over 2,600 locations and annual sales exceeding $10 billion.

Prioritizing People Over Profits

"Success is not final; failure is not fatal: It is the courage to continue that counts." - Winston Churchill.

Truett Cathy's business philosophy was deeply rooted in his faith and values. Chick-fil-A restaurants are closed on Sundays, allowing employees to rest and spend time with their families, a practice that remains a cornerstone of the company's culture. Cathy's belief in serving others extended beyond his customers to his employees, whom he viewed as integral to the company's success.

Generosity is a Mindset and not a Bank Account!

"Real generosity toward the future lies in giving all to the present." – Albert Camus.

Truett Cathy's commitment to philanthropy is as impressive as his business success. Through the Leadership Scholarship program for Chick-fil-A employees, more than $23 million has been awarded in scholarships over the past 35 years, empowering young people to pursue their educational dreams.

In 1984, Cathy established the WinShape Foundation, with a mission to shape winners. This foundation has provided support for numerous programs, including summer camps, foster homes, and marriage retreats, reflecting Cathy's dedication to strengthening families and communities.

Fostering Hope and Opportunity

"Life's most persistent and urgent question is, 'What are you doing for others?'" – Dr. Martin Luther King Jr.

For more than 30 years, Truett Cathy and his wife fostered children, providing a loving home and opportunities for a better future. This personal commitment to nurturing young lives is a testament to Cathy's belief in the power of giving and service.

Legacy of Impact

"Legacy is not what I do for myself. It's what I'm doing for the next generation." – Vitor Belfort.

Truett Cathy's story is more than just a tale of business success; it's a powerful narrative of how living your dream with purpose and compassion can lead to a life of true significance. His unwavering commitment to faith, family, and philanthropy serves as an inspiration for us all to pursue our dreams with passion and purpose, and to use our success to make a difference in the lives of others.

Living your dream and sowing seeds that benefit others is the key to a life of significance. Truett Cathy's journey from a $10,400 loan to a billion-dollar empire is a shining example of living life big. His dedication to his employees, his philanthropic endeavors, and his commitment to fostering children demonstrate that true success is measured by the positive impact we have on the world around us.

As you embark on your own journey, remember the words of Truett Cathy: "We change the world, and ourselves, by our response to unexpected opportunities." By embracing opportunities to serve others, we can all live a life of significance and leave a legacy.

Missionaries of Charity Fonder, Mother Teresa: A Beacon of Compassion and Humanity

"Not all of us can do great things. But we can do small things with great love." – Mother Teresa.

Mother Teresa, born Anjezë Gonxhe Bojaxhiu in 1910 in Skopje, North Macedonia, dedicated her life to serving the poorest of the poor. She founded the Missionaries of Charity in 1950 in Calcutta, India, with a mission to care for the "hungry, the naked, the homeless, the crippled, the blind, the lepers, all those people who feel unwanted, unloved, uncared for throughout society, people that have become a burden to the society and are shunned by everyone."

Her selfless dedication to others earned her the Nobel Peace Prize in 1979. Mother Teresa's legacy lives on through the thousands of Missionaries of Charity members who continue her work worldwide. Her famous words, "Not all of us can do great things. But we can do small things with great love," encapsulates her belief in the power of small acts of kindness.

Impact on the World

Mother Teresa's work has had a profound impact on the world, providing a model of unconditional love and care for the marginalized. The Missionaries of Charity operate in over 130 countries, running homes for people dying of HIV/AIDS, leprosy, and tuberculosis, and providing soup kitchens, dispensaries, and mobile clinics. Her life of significance, marked by her relentless commitment to helping those in need, continues to inspire millions.

Mahatma Gandhi: The Architect of Peaceful Resistance

Champion of Nonviolent Protest

Mahatma Gandhi, born Mohandas Karamchand Gandhi in 1869 in Porbandar, India, is renowned for leading India to independence through nonviolent civil disobedience. He believed in "Satyagraha," a philosophy that advocated for truth and nonviolence as powerful tools for social change. Gandhi's dream was to see an India free from British rule, achieved through peaceful means.

His famous quote, "The best way to find yourself is to lose yourself in the service of others," reflects his belief in living a life of significance. Through his leadership in the Indian independence movement, Gandhi not only achieved his dream but also set a precedent for future social justice movements worldwide.

Global Influence

Gandhi's methods of peaceful protest have inspired countless leaders and movements, including the Civil Rights Movement in the United States. His impact on the world is immeasurable, as he demonstrated that enduring change is possible through nonviolence and selflessness. Gandhi's legacy continues to guide activists and leaders in their fight for justice and equality.

Dr. Nelson Mandela: Champion of Freedom

"What counts in life is not the mere fact that we have lived. It is what difference we have made to the lives of others that will determine the significance of the life we lead." – Nelson Mandela.

Nelson Rolihlahla Mandela, born on July 18, 1918, in Mvezo, South Africa, devoted his life to the fight against apartheid—a brutal system of racial segregation. Mandela's dream was a democratic and free society where all people lived together in harmony with equal opportunities. Despite being imprisoned for 27 years, Mandela never wavered in his pursuit of justice and equality.

Upon his release in 1990, Mandela led negotiations to dismantle apartheid, culminating in his election as South Africa's first black president in 1994. His leadership and reconciliation efforts earned him the Nobel Peace Prize in 1993. Mandela's life is a testament to the power of resilience, forgiveness, and the enduring fight for human rights.

Harriet Tubman: The Liberator of the Oppressed

The Moses of Her People

Harriet Tubman, born Araminta Ross around 1822 in Dorchester County, Maryland, escaped slavery and became a leading abolitionist and conductor of the Underground Railroad. Tubman risked her life to lead hundreds of enslaved people to freedom, earning her the nickname "Moses" for her role in guiding her people to liberation.

Her words, "Every great dream begins with a dreamer. Always remember, you have within you the strength, the patience, and the passion to reach for the stars to change the world," highlight her unwavering determination and courage. Tubman's dream was not only to secure her own freedom but to free others from the bonds of slavery.

Impact on American History

Harriet Tubman's legacy is one of bravery and relentless pursuit of justice. Her work during the Civil War as a spy, scout, and nurse for the Union Army further exemplifies her dedication to the fight for freedom. Tubman's life of significance is a testament to the power of one individual's courage and determination to bring about monumental change.

These remarkable individuals—Mother Teresa, Mahatma Gandhi, Nelson Mandela, Dr. Martin Luther King Jr., and Harriet Tubman—demonstrated that living life big involves pursuing dreams with a mindset of significance. By putting others first and dedicating themselves to causes greater than themselves, they left an indelible mark on the world, inspiring generations to strive for justice, equality, and compassion.

How to Identify and Pursue Your True Dream

1. **Self-Reflection**: Spend time understanding what genuinely excites and motivates you. Reflect on moments when you felt most alive and engaged.

2. **Listen to Your Inner Voice**: Pay attention to your intuition and inner desires. They often guide you toward your true path.

3. **Seek Authenticity**: Surround yourself with people and experiences that encourage you to be your authentic self.

4. **Set Personal Goals**: Define what success looks like for you, independent of societal or familial expectations.

5. **Embrace Change**: Be open to evolving your dreams as you grow. What was once your passion may shift, and that's perfectly okay.

Ensuring that you live your own dream is crucial for a fulfilling and meaningful life. When you live your dream, life transforms from a burdensome obligation into a journey of endless possibilities and profound satisfaction. So, take a moment, introspect, and make sure the dream you're pursuing is truly yours. Embrace your unique path, and let it lead you to a life of joy and fulfillment.

Self-Activity for Chapter Two.

"The best effect of any book is that it excites the reader to self-activity." – Thomas Carlyle.

To bring the power of living your own dream into focus, reflect on these engaging questions. Answer them honestly, and let your responses guide you toward practical actions.

1. **What's Your Dream?**
   Think about a dream that excites you. What passion have you had that feels uniquely yours, untainted by external expectations? Write it down.

2. **Why Haven't You Pursued It Fully?**
   Be honest. Is it fear of failure, lack of time, or fear of judgment? What's the main barrier holding you back?

3. **What Would Happen If You Didn't Quit?**
   Imagine how your life might change if you are committed to your dream for the next five years. What potential impact could you make by staying resilient?

4. **Who Inspires You to Keep Going?**
   Think of someone who never gave up on their dream, whether it's Elon Musk, Nelson Mandela, or someone personal. How can you use their story as motivation?

5. **What Small Step Can You Take Today?**
   Success begins with small, consistent actions. What can you do today to move closer to living your dream? Make it practical, simple, and achievable.

As you engage with these questions, take note of how your mindset shifts. Let them spark excitement and clarity as you continue your journey to live life big!

CHAPTER THREE:
DON'T LEAVE YOUR DREAM, LIVE YOUR DREAM!

"The greatest tragedy in life is not death, but a life without a purpose." – Dr. Myles Munroe.

A Dreamer's Dilemma: The Cost of Aspiration

Life often presents dreams as shimmering beacons, guiding us toward a future full of promises. Yet, what it fails to reveal is the steep price those dreams demand. The pursuit of your dream is not for the faint hearted; it's a path laden with challenges, sacrifices, and moments of perplexing doubts and profound dilemma. But without the magnetic pull of that dream, few would willingly walk the arduous journey it requires.

David Tolu Oridota found himself at such a crossroads, where the cost of pursuing his dream seemed overwhelming. He faced ridicule, alienation, and the loss of respect from friends, family, and even his community— all because he dared to chase something greater. But David's story is not one of surrender; it's a testament to the power of living your dream, no matter the obstacles.

David Tolu Oridota`s Story - A Clash of Destinies: Medicine or Music?

"The biggest adventure you can take is to live the life of your dreams." — Oprah Winfrey.

Growing up in a loving, faith-filled family, David's path seemed predestined. His father, a gynecologist, and his mother, a nurse, were pillars of strength, providing the best for their children. As the eldest, David was expected to follow a prestigious career in medicine, a choice that would make his parents proud. Yet, a different rhythm called to him—music. The pull was undeniable, stronger than the logical path laid out before him.

The Struggle Within: A Dream Deferred

David's journey into medical school in Nigeria marked the beginning of an internal battle. As his peers immersed themselves in studies, David's passion for music only grew stronger. Music was not just a hobby; it was a lifeline, a connection to his true self. Despite the pressure to conform, David couldn't ignore the voice within urging him to live his dream.

After much contemplation, David made a bold decision: he would defer his Medical Board examination and pursue a degree in Music Merchandising at the prestigious Berklee College of Music. But this decision was met with fierce resistance, particularly from his father. The conflict escalated, leading to ridicule from his community and alienation from his family. Yet, through it all, the joy he found in music sustained him.

A Compromise with Destiny: Engineering a New Path

Unable to gain his family's approval to study music, David struck a compromise—he would study Computer Engineering at the University of Kansas in the USA. This decision was not a retreat from his passion but an acknowledgment of his diverse talents. David had always excelled in computer programming, and he realized that life offers multiple avenues to fulfill one's destiny.

A Leap of Faith: Turning Music into a Lifeline

As David settled into his new path, a call from his father threatened to derail everything. His father's financial support was running out, and David was left with only $5,000 to his name. Faced with the prospect of dropping out of school and being evicted from his apartment, David made a daring move. He invested $4,500 in a Korg Triton 88-key Music WorkStation, betting everything on his musical talent.

Armed with his new workstation, David began sequencing popular worship songs, creating full orchestrations that could pass for live bands. His one-man band quickly gained attention, and soon, churches across the country were inviting him to play. David's gift made room for him, leading to opportunities he had never imagined.

The Breakthrough: A Contract of a Lifetime

"Don't be pushed around by the fears in your mind. Be led by the dreams in your heart." — Roy T. Bennett.

David's persistence and innovation paid off when he landed a $500,000 contract to provide music for the military. This opportunity not only saved his educational journey but also allowed him to hire other musicians and expand his impact. David returned to school, earning degrees in Electronics Engineering and an MBA in Information Systems. Today, as the Principal Software

Engineer for a successful startup, David's story is a powerful example of what it means to live your dream.

Reconnecting with Destiny: A Full Circle Moment

David's story is deeply personal to me. We were classmates at the University of Ibadan, West Africa's premier university, where I graduated as a medical doctor in 2005. For many years, we lost touch, and I often wondered where life had taken him, especially after knowing about the conflict he had with his father that led him to leave medical school prematurely.

About two years ago, while reading "Put Your Dream to the Test" by my mentor, Dr. John Maxwell, David came to mind. My curiosity led me to search for him, and after much effort, I found his contact and reconnected. I'm so glad I can share his story in this book with his kind permission.

Living Your Dream: The Rules of Engagement

David's journey is a powerful reminder that every aspect of creation is designed for success. Just as birds are meant to fly and fish to swim, you are meant to thrive in your God-given purpose. But to do so, you must find and follow the rules of engagement that guide you towards your fulfillment. Don't leave your dream—live it and watch as success unfolds in your life.

"Your time is limited, so don't waste it living someone else's life. Have the courage to follow your heart and intuition." — Steve Jobs.

David Tolu Oridota's story is more than an inspiration; it's a living blueprint for anyone daring to live their dream. His journey teaches us that while the road may be challenging, the rewards of staying true to your purpose are immeasurable.

Dr. Martin Luther King Jr. - The Man Behind the Dream of a New Nation!

On August 28, 1963, a day forever etched in the annals of history, Dr. Martin Luther King Jr. stood resolutely in front of the Lincoln Memorial. As he gazed over the sea of troubled Americans who had gathered in the name of civil rights, he uttered the now immortal words, "I have a dream." This was not just a speech; it was a dream birthed in the heart of a man daring enough to think the unthinkable and see the invisible, because he believed it was possible.

From Humble Beginnings to a Grand Vision

Dr. Martin Luther King Jr. was born on January 15, 1929, in Atlanta, Georgia, into a family deeply rooted in the church and the struggle for racial equality. His father, Martin Luther King Sr., was a Baptist minister and a strong advocate for civil rights, and his mother, Alberta Williams King, was a schoolteacher. Young Martin grew up in an environment where the values of education, justice, and faith were paramount.

Despite the oppressive racial segregation of the time, King excelled in his studies, skipping two grades and entering Morehouse College at the age of 15. His journey to becoming a beacon of hope for millions was fueled by a combination of intellectual rigor, spiritual depth, and a profound sense of justice. Inspired by the teachings of Mahatma Gandhi and the nonviolent resistance movement, King began to see a way to transform his dream of equality and justice into reality.

The Dream That Changed the World!

Dr. King's dream was not a sudden revelation but a culmination of years of struggle, observation, and deep reflection. His dream was a response to the cries of the oppressed, a vision where "justice rolls down like waters and righteousness like a mighty stream." This dream was vividly articulated in his "I Have a Dream" speech, where he envisioned a world where people would "not be judged by the color of their skin but by the content of their character."

His words resonated far beyond the steps of the Lincoln Memorial, igniting a movement that would lead to significant legislative and social changes.

A Dream of Equality

Voice of the Civil Rights Movement

King's powerful statement, "Life's most persistent and urgent question is, 'What are you doing for others?'" epitomizes his commitment to a life of significance. His leadership in civil rights resulted in landmark legislation, including the Civil Rights Act of 1964 and the Voting Rights Act of 1965, which dismantled institutionalized racial segregation and discrimination.

Enduring Legacy

Dr. King's influence extends far beyond his lifetime. His work laid the foundation for continued progress in civil rights and social justice. His commitment to equality, justice, and nonviolence continues to inspire and mobilize individuals and movements worldwide, proving the enduring power of living one's dream with a focus on significance.

The Power of Living Your Dream

"If you dream of becoming an eagle, you follow your dreams and not the words of a bunch of chickens." – Penny Johnson Jerald.

Imagine if Dr. Martin Luther King Jr. had chosen to leave his dream instead of living it. The world would have missed out on a transformative leader whose vision redefined the fabric of society. The consequences of abandoning (leaving) one's dreams can be dire, not just for the individual but for the world at large. Dreams left unpursued represent lost opportunities for innovation, novelty, creativity, compassion, and progress. Dr. John Maxwell has been called the #1 leader in business and the most influential leadership expert in the world. He said, "The only tragedy worse than dying with dreams unfulfilled is never to have dreamed at all."

The Graveyard of Unsung Dreams

"The graveyard is the richest place on Earth," mused author Dr. Myles Munroe, "because it is here that you will find all the hopes and dreams that were never fulfilled, the books that were never written, the songs that were never sung, the inventions that were never shared, the cures that were never discovered, all because someone was too afraid to take that first step, keep with the problem, or determined to carry out their dream."

The Impact of Living Your Dream

Living your dream is not just about personal fulfillment; it is about making a significant impact on the world. As Steve Jobs famously said, "The people who are crazy enough to think they can change the world are the ones who do." By daring to live his dream, Dr. Martin Luther King Jr. changed the course of history and improved the lives of countless individuals.

Each of us harbors dreams that have the potential to bring about positive change. Whether it's a dream to start a business, write a book, or advocate for a cause, living our dreams can inspire and uplift others. As Eleanor Roosevelt put it, "The future belongs to those who believe in the beauty of their dreams."

Embrace Your Dream

To truly "Live Life Big," one must embrace their dreams with passion and determination. It's about overcoming fear, resisting complacency, and pushing through obstacles. Living your dream means believing in its possibility and taking actionable steps to make it a reality. It's about daring to be different and persevering in the face of adversity. Dr. Martin Luther King Jr.'s journey teaches us that living our dreams is not only possible but essential for the betterment of society.

Dare to Live Your Dream!

As we reflect on the life and legacy of Dr. Martin Luther King Jr., we are reminded of the profound impact one individual's dream can have on the world. His story is a testament to the power of living one's dream and the transformative effect it can have on society. Let us all be inspired to live life big—don't leave your dream, live your dream!

The world needs your unique contributions, and it is through the pursuit of our dreams that we can create a better, more just, and more beautiful world. As you embark on your journey, remember the words of Johann Wolfgang von Goethe: "Whatever you can do or dream you can, begin it. Boldness has genius, power, and magic in it." Let us all dare to dream, and more importantly, dare to live those dreams.

From White Coats to Life-Changing Impact: My Journey to Living My Dream

"You are either leaving or living your dream. Leaving your dream dims your world; living it brightens your universe." – Dr. Michael Koku.

The Beauty of Dreams: A Childhood Aspiration

"The future belongs to those who believe in the beauty of their dreams." - Eleanor Roosevelt.

From a young age, my dream was clear: I wanted to become a medical doctor. Frequent visits to the hospital due to numerous playground injuries sparked a fascination with the medical profession. Growing up, I envisioned myself wearing a white coat, respected in society, and dedicated to healing.

Stretching for My Childhood Aspiration: The Journey to Medical School

With determination and hard work, I made it to medical school. It felt like the culmination of my lifelong ambition. But as I delved deeper into my studies, I began to sense a greater calling within me. My desire to help people remained strong, yet I realized there was more to my purpose than being a doctor.

Unveiling a Greater Purpose

I discovered that my true dream was to add measurable value to human lives, helping others reach their full potential and become the best versions of themselves. This epiphany transformed my life. While I still cherished the idea of caring for people, my vision expanded to include inspiring and empowering others on a broader scale.

Living the Dream: A Commitment to Impact

"The best way to find yourself is to lose yourself in the service of others." - Mahatma Gandhi.

Today, I am living my dream and understand what true significance looks like. To live life big, it's not enough to have a dream—you must take ownership of it. This means investing your time, talent, and resources in actively pursuing your passion.

The Difference Between Believing and Owning Your Dream

There are many who believe in their dreams, but few who truly take ownership of them. When you don't own your dream, it's easy to abandon it. But when you invest in your dream through sacrifice and self-investment, you become dedicated to it. This commitment ensures you will cleave to your dream, live it fully, and ultimately live life big.

Don't Leave Your Dream, Live Your Dream

"For all sad words of tongue or pen, the saddest are these: 'It might have been.'" - John Greenleaf Whittier.

Dare to dream and dare even more to own your dream. It is in this ownership that you will find the strength to overcome obstacles, the resilience to stand firm against the status quo, and the joy of living a life of true impact. Live your dream, live life big, and inspire others to do the same. Don't Leave Your Dream, Live Your Dream!

Self-Activity for *Chapter Three.*

Engage with these thought-provoking questions to reflect on your commitment to your dreams. Use them to reignite your passion and identify practical steps to ensure you're living, not leaving, your dream.

1. **What Dream Are You Leaving Behind?** Is there a dream you've abandoned or put aside? What was it, and why did you leave it behind?

2. **What Would It Take to Reclaim It?** What actions or mindset shifts would help you start

living your dream again? What is the first small step you can take today?

3. **Who or What Is Holding You Back?**
Identify any barriers—people, fears, or circumstances—that are stopping you from living your dream. How can you overcome them?

4. **What Would Happen If You Fully Lived Your Dream?**
Imagine how your life would change if you fully pursued your dream. What impact could you make on your life and the lives of others?

5. **What Legacy Do You Want to Leave?**
When you think about your future, what legacy will living your dream leave behind? How can you start building that legacy now?

These questions are designed to challenge your current mindset and inspire action. Let them guide you toward actively living your dream!

CHAPTER FOUR
IT IS NEVER TOO LATE TO LIVE YOUR DREAM!

"The best time to plant a tree was 20 years ago. The second-best time is now." – Chinese Proverb.

Dreams are the fuel that keeps us alive, pushing us beyond the ordinary and into the extraordinary. Yet, so often, we find ourselves sidelining our dreams, making excuses that rob us of the joy and fulfillment that comes from pursuing them. **"He that is good for making excuses is seldom good for anything else,"** Benjamin Franklin once said, emphasizing how excuses can become the chains that bind us to mediocrity.

Excuses: The Dream Killers

George Washington Carver wisely observed that **"Ninety-nine percent of the failures come from people who have the habit of making excuses."** Excuses may comfort us temporarily, but as Mason Cooley pointed out, they **"change nothing, but make everyone feel better."** They are the barriers we create to shield ourselves from the fear of failure or the discomfort of stepping out of our comfort zones. However, if there is breath in your lungs, there is still time to live your dream. **"It is never too late to be what you might have been,"** wrote George Eliot, reminding us that our dreams are still within reach, no matter how delayed.

Dreams Are Timeless, But Some Are Time-Sensitive

While it's true that certain dreams, like becoming an Olympian, are time-sensitive, many dreams are not bound by age. The key is to start as early as possible because the sooner you begin, the more time you have to grow, evolve, and make an impact. But even if you start late, you can still achieve incredible things. Here are two remarkable stories that prove age is not a barrier to living your dreams.

1. A New Era of Beauty: Marissa Teijo, 71, Competes in Miss Texas USA

"Age is an issue of mind over matter. If you don't mind, it doesn't matter." – Mark Twain.

Marissa Teijo, at 71 years old, made history as the oldest contestant ever to compete in the Miss Texas USA pageant in 2024. Following a recent rule change that removed age limits, Teijo seized the opportunity to fulfill a lifelong dream. She didn't just participate; she inspired countless others by proving that beauty and ambition don't fade with time. "**I hope to inspire women to strive to be their best physical and mental self and believe there is beauty at any age,**" she shared, radiating confidence and grace.

Her journey was not just about walking the runway but about walking the path of courage, defying stereotypes, and showing that every stage of life is a stage of opportunity, strength, and beauty. "**The future belongs to those who believe in the beauty of their dreams,**" said Eleanor Roosevelt, and Teijo's story is a testament to that truth.

2. A Dream Fulfilled After 83 Years: Virginia 'Ginger' Hislop, 105, Earns Her Master's Degree

"It is not true that people stop pursuing their dreams because they grow old, they grow old because they stop pursuing their dreams." – Gabriel Garcia Marquez.

At the astonishing age of 105, Virginia "Ginger" Hislop returned to Stanford University to complete her master's degree, a dream she had put on hold for over 80 years. Her journey began in 1936, but life's circumstances—marriage, World War II, and a fulfilling career—delayed her goal. Yet, Hislop never let go of her dream. In June 2024, surrounded by her grandchildren and great-grandchildren, she finally walked across the stage to receive her diploma.

"My goodness," she exclaimed, reflecting on her achievement. **"I've waited a long time for this."** Her story is a powerful reminder that it's never too late to pursue your dreams. **"You are never too old to set another goal or to dream a new dream,"** said C.S. Lewis, and Hislop's journey embodies this belief. Her perseverance and dedication to education are a beacon of hope for anyone who thinks time has passed by.

Start Now: No More Excuses

"Do not wait to strike till the iron is hot, but make it hot by striking." – William Butler Yeats.

The stories of Marissa Teijo and Virginia Hislop serve as powerful reminders that excuses are the enemy of dreams. It's easy to say, "I'm too old," "It's too late," or "I don't have enough time," but the truth is that the only thing standing between you and your dream is the story you tell yourself. If you are breathing, there is still time to make your dream a reality. **"You are never too old to reinvent yourself,"** Oprah Winfrey said, and now is the perfect time to start.

So, what's holding you back? **"The only limit to our realization of tomorrow will be our doubts of today,"** warned Franklin D. Roosevelt. Let go of the excuses, embrace your dreams, and remember: **"The future depends on what you do today."** – Mahatma Gandhi. Start now, because it is never too late to live your dream!

Living Your Dream Beyond 50: The Remarkable Stories of Ray Kroc and Colonel Sanders

"Success is not final; failure is not fatal: It is the courage to continue that counts." – Winston Churchill.

Success knows no age limit. While many believe that dreams are the domain of the young, two of the most iconic figures in American business history, Ray Kroc of McDonald's and Colonel Harland Sanders of Kentucky Fried Chicken, defied this notion. They didn't just live their dreams; they revolutionized entire industries—proving that it's never too late to embark on your journey to greatness.

Ray Kroc: The Visionary Who Transformed McDonald's into a Global Giant

"The only way to do great work is to love what you do." – Steve Jobs.

Raymond Albert Kroc was already 52 years old when he first encountered a small but remarkably efficient hamburger stand in San Bernardino, California. It was 1954, and Kroc was a struggling milkshake mixer salesman when he stumbled upon the restaurant owned by Richard and Maurice McDonald. The brothers had perfected a system that produced high-quality food with astonishing speed. Kroc, with his keen business acumen, immediately recognized the potential of this concept.

But he didn't just see a successful restaurant; he saw a global empire. **"It's not what you look at that matters, it's what you see,"** said Henry David Thoreau, and Kroc saw the future. Convincing the McDonald brothers to allow him to franchise their concept, he embarked on a journey that would redefine the fast-food industry.

Under Kroc's leadership, McDonald's became a household name. He implemented groundbreaking innovations such as a standardized menu and an assembly-line system that ensured consistency and efficiency across all locations. **"Innovation distinguishes between a leader and a follower,"** said Steve Jobs, and Kroc was undoubtedly a leader.

By 1961, Kroc had bought out the McDonald brothers for $2.7 million, taking full control of the company. From then on, he pursued aggressive expansion, turning McDonald's into the most successful fast-food corporation in the world by revenue. His relentless drive and visionary approach transformed a small hamburger stand into a global phenomenon, proving that **it's never too late to be what you might have been.**

Colonel Sanders: The Man Who Fried His Way to the Top at 65

"**Your age doesn't define your ability to accomplish great things.**" – Anonymous.

Harland David Sanders, better known as Colonel Sanders, was 65 years old when he finally achieved the success that had eluded him for decades. Born in 1890, Sanders had a rough start in life. He held numerous jobs, from steam engine stoker to insurance salesman, but nothing seemed to stick. It wasn't until the Great Depression that Sanders found his calling: fried chicken.

In North Corbin, Kentucky, Sanders began selling fried chicken from a roadside restaurant. He had developed a secret recipe and a patented pressure-frying method that made his chicken irresistible. Yet, despite his culinary breakthrough, Sanders struggled to keep his restaurant afloat. "**Success is not the key to happiness. Happiness is the key to success. If you love what you are doing, you will be successful,**" said Albert Schweitzer, and Sanders loved his chicken, even when the odds were against him.

In 1952, at the age of 62, Sanders began franchising his chicken concept, opening the first Kentucky Fried Chicken (KFC) franchise in South Salt Lake, Utah. The response was overwhelming, and by 1964, KFC had grown so rapidly that Sanders sold the company for $2 million—equivalent to $19.6 million today. But even after selling the company, Sanders continued to serve as KFC's brand ambassador, embodying the spirit of the business well into his later years.

Colonel Sanders' journey is a testament to the power of persistence and passion. **"It does not matter how slowly you go as long as you do not stop,"** Confucius said, and Sanders never stopped, not even when faced with failure after failure. His legacy is a powerful reminder that it's never too late to fry up your dreams and serve them to the world.

Age Is Just a Number: The Time to Start Is Now

"The only limits to our realization of tomorrow are our doubts of today." – Franklin D. Roosevelt.

Ray Kroc and Colonel Sanders are shining examples that it's never too late to live your dream. Their stories are not just about building businesses; they are about the indomitable human spirit, the courage to start over, and the belief that the best is yet to come. **"You are never too old to set another goal or to dream a new dream,"** said C.S. Lewis, and these men proved that age is not a barrier but a steppingstone to greatness.

So, if you're thinking it's too late to pursue your passion, remember Ray Kroc and Colonel Sanders. They didn't just dream; they lived their dreams, turning them into legacies that continue to inspire millions. **"It's never too late to be what you might have been,"** George Eliot reminds us.

The time to start is now. Your dream is waiting for you to make it a reality.

Self-Activity for *Chapter Four*

Use these powerful questions to reflect on where you are in your journey and reignite your passion for pursuing your dream, no matter your age or stage of life.

1. **What Dream Have You Put Aside?**
   Is there a dream you once cherished but set aside? What stopped you from pursuing it?

2. **What Excuses Have You Made?**
   Be honest—what excuses have kept you from chasing your dream? How can you overcome those excuses today?

3. **What Would It Mean to Live Your Dream Now?**
   How would your life change if you started pursuing your dream right now? What impact would it have on your happiness, purpose, and legacy?

4. **What Small Step Can You Take Today?**
   Every dream starts with one action. What is one small, manageable step you can take today to begin living your dream?

5. **Who Can You Look to for Inspiration?**
   Think of someone who achieved success later in life. How can their journey inspire and motivate you to start now?

Reflect on these questions to spark the action needed to begin living your dream—it's never too late!

CHAPTER FIVE
YOUR DREAM IS NOT ABOUT YOU—IT'S ABOUT OTHERS!

"Your reward in life will be in direct proportion to the value of your service to others." – Brian Tracy.

On a cold Christmas Eve in 1910, the beloved founder of The Salvation Army, General William Booth, lay frail and nearing the end of his life. Although he could not physically attend the Army's annual convention, his spirit of service and dedication to others remained strong. As a gesture of encouragement to the thousands of Salvation Army soldiers gathered at the convention, who were tirelessly serving the needy during the harsh winter months, it was suggested that General Booth send a telegram.

Funds were tight, and telegrams were charged by the word, so Booth had to choose his words carefully. What message could capture the essence of his life, the mission of The Salvation Army, and the spirit of service? He pondered deeply, reflecting on his decades of ministry and service, searching for the one word that encapsulated everything he stood for.

When the delegates gathered at the convention, the atmosphere was heavy with concern and uncertainty, knowing their beloved leader could not be present. The moderator stood up to announce the reason for Booth's absence and to share the telegram that Booth had sent. As the room fell silent, the moderator opened the telegram and read aloud the single, profound word:

"Others!"

That one word, "Others," resonated throughout the convention hall like a clarion call, immediately lifting the spirits of everyone present. It perfectly encapsulated Booth's lifelong commitment to serving others and the core mission of The Salvation Army. For Booth, and for all those who have ever dedicated their lives to serving others, the dream was never about personal gain or glory; it was always about lifting others up, making a difference in the lives of those in need, and sowing seeds of compassion and kindness.

A Legacy of Service and Impact

William Booth's life and mission were grounded in this principle of living for others. Born into poverty in Sneinton, Nottingham, in 1829, Booth experienced firsthand the harsh realities of life. His early years were marked by financial struggles after his father's death. Apprentice to a pawnbroker at the age of 13, Booth became acutely aware of the injustices faced by the poor. These experiences shaped his resolve to dedicate his life to helping the marginalized and the destitute.

His journey was not easy. General Booth faced countless challenges, from financial hardships to opposition from established religious institutions. Yet, he never wavered in his commitment to his calling. Inspired by his deep faith, he believed in the transformative power of the Gospel and its capacity to change lives—not just spiritually, but also socially and economically. Booth's vision was to create a movement that went beyond the church walls, directly addressing the needs of the poor and downtrodden.

"While women weep, as they do now, I'll fight; while little children go hungry, I'll fight; while men go to prison, in and out, in and out, as they do now, I'll fight; while there is a drunkard left, while there is a poor lost girl upon the streets, where there remains one dark soul without the light of God, I'll fight—I'll fight to the very end!" — William Booth.

This was the relentless spirit of Booth and The Salvation Army. His dream was never about personal comfort or prestige but about fighting for others, advocating for the helpless, and bringing hope where there was none.

Dreams That Serve Others

Booth's life is a powerful reminder that our dreams and aspirations are not just about us. They are about the impact we have on others—the lives we touch, the communities we uplift, and the legacy we leave behind. Our dreams find their true purpose when they are aligned with serving others. When we pursue dreams that benefit humanity, we sow seeds of hope, kindness, and love that can grow far beyond what we could ever imagine.

"Success is not what you have done compared to what others have done. Success is what you have done compared to what you were created to do." — Dr. John Maxwell.

William Booth's dream was to create a movement that would bring practical help and spiritual hope to those who needed it most. By the end of his life, The Salvation Army had spread to 58 countries, providing food, shelter, and spiritual support to millions. The legacy of Booth's dream continues to thrive today, over a century later, touching countless lives worldwide.

Live Your Dream to Serve Others

In living our dreams, we must remember that it is not about us. It is about the others who will benefit from our efforts and the positive change we can bring to the world. Whether in small acts of kindness or in grand gestures of generosity, the dreams that truly matter are those that reach beyond us and contribute to the well-being of others.

As you pursue your dreams, let the story of William Booth and his one-word telegram inspire you. Dream big, but dream with others in mind. Live a life of purpose and service and know that your greatest fulfillment will come not from what you achieve for yourself, but from what you do for others.

"We make a living by what we get, but we make a life by what we give." — Winston Churchill.

Just like Booth, let your life be a testament to the power of dreaming for others. May your dreams always be fueled by a desire to serve, uplift, and empower those around you. After all, it is in giving that we truly receive, and it is in living for others that we find our deepest sense of purpose and fulfillment.

The Heart of Integrity: A Tale of Two House Surgeons

During my internship as a house surgeon in the oncology unit, I encountered a profound lesson in ethics and integrity—one that has stayed with me throughout my career. One of my consultants, an esteemed oncologist who now serves as the provost of the College of Medicine at my alma mater, shared a deeply troubling story. It was a true account of a former house surgeon in our unit who betrayed the trust placed in him and jeopardized a patient's life.

In our unit, patients could choose from three different chemotherapy options, depending on their financial capabilities. At that time, health insurance was practically nonexistent in Nigerian Federal Teaching Hospitals, making patients to pay 100% out-of-pocket. This patient could afford the most effective, albeit expensive, chemotherapy treatment, which promised the best outcomes.

However, the house surgeon, entrusted with the care of this patient, chose to administer placebo (injection water) instead of the prescribed chemotherapy medication. He documented in the patient's file that the correct medication was given—a despicable act of deceit and fraud. As the saying goes, "Your sins will find you out."

Deceit Unveiled: When Integrity is Compromised

How did this malpractice come to light? After every chemotherapy cycle, standard procedure requires post-treatment blood work to assess the medication's impact. The results for this patient were far below expectations, leading the oncologist to suspect something was amiss. The oncologist confronted the corrupt house surgeon, who eventually confessed to malpractice, revealing his plan to sell the actual medication to another patient. This act of selfishness and betrayal was met with swift justice, as his medical license was suspended.

Simon Sinek, a renowned author, speaker, and optimist, once said, "It is a luxury to put our interests first. It is an honor to put the interests of others before our own." This resonates deeply in the context of this story. The house surgeon's actions were a stark reminder that our dreams and goals should never come at the expense of others. His selfishness not only harmed the patient but also tarnished the trust that patients place in their healthcare providers.

BELOVED PHYSICIANS: A Mission to Serve

My own journey as a house physician was shaped by a different vision—a vision that placed others at the forefront. During my one-year mandatory internship, I founded a group called **BELOVED PHYSICIANS**, comprising house officers—both physicians and surgeons. We met weekly to support each other and grow together in our faith, finances, relationships, and career pursuits.

Driven by a desire to make a meaningful difference, we pooled our resources and rallied like-minded individuals to help patients who couldn't afford healthcare. We purchased essential items such as medications, sterilizers, sphygmomanometers, hospital screens, and mattresses for mothers staying overnight with their children in the hospital. Our mission didn't stop there; we identified needs in various wards that hindered optimal patient care and donated necessary supplies to the hospital authorities, capturing their attention and support.

We also initiated an annual award ceremony [TABITHA NITE] to celebrate staff members who went above and beyond to positively impact healthcare within the system. Our efforts were a testament to the belief that **our dreams** are not about us—they're about what we can do for others.

The Ripple Effect of Selfless Service

Bernard Meltzer, a beloved American radio host, once said, "There is no better exercise for your heart than reaching down and helping to lift someone up." This sentiment perfectly encapsulates the spirit of BELOVED PHYSICIANS. Our dream was not just to excel in our medical careers but to use our positions to make a positive impact on the lives of those we served.

In every profession, we face choices that test our integrity. We can choose the path of self-interest, as the deceitful house surgeon did, or we can choose the path of selflessness, as we did with BELOVED PHYSICIANS. The latter path, though challenging, leads to a more profound life and legacy. It's a journey that brings meaning not only to our lives but to the lives of countless others.

Our Dreams Fulfilled Through the Service of Others

Ultimately, the stories we remember and share are not those of personal gain or glory but of the times we reached beyond ourselves to lift someone else. Let us remember that **our dreams are not about us—they are about the impact we have on the world around us**. When we live with that mindset, we create a ripple effect of positivity and change that can touch lives far beyond our own.

Albert Schweitzer: A Life of Service and Compassion

Albert Schweitzer, a name synonymous with selfless service, beautifully encapsulates the essence of living a dream not for oneself but for the benefit of others. He famously said, **"The purpose of human life is to serve, and to show compassion and the will to help others."** This philosophy guided his entire life, driving him to sacrifice personal comfort and professional accolades to pursue a higher calling: serving humanity. Schweitzer's life is a powerful testament to the idea that the true measure of our dreams lies in the impact they have on the world around us.

Answering the Call: A Dream Beyond Self

At the age of 30, Albert Schweitzer answered a call that would forever change his life and the lives of countless others. Despite his impressive credentials as a theologian, organist, and musicologist, he felt an undeniable pull toward medicine. He chose to study medicine with the goal of going to Africa to provide healthcare in areas with little to no access. This decision was not made lightly. It meant giving up a prestigious career and starting anew in a field where he had no experience. As he put it, **"I don't know what your destiny will be, but one thing I know: the only ones among you who will be really happy are those who will have sought and found how to serve."** His dream was not about personal gain or recognition but about a commitment to others—a choice that brought both challenges and immense fulfillment.

Building the Dream: The Hôpital Albert Schweitzer

In 1913, Schweitzer and his wife, Helene, embarked on a journey to establish the Hôpital Albert Schweitzer in Lambaréné, in what is now Gabon. They were driven by a vision to serve, grounded in Schweitzer's philosophy of

"**Reverence for Life.**" This hospital was more than just a medical facility; it was a manifestation of Schweitzer's belief in the sanctity of all life and his commitment to alleviating suffering wherever he could.

The early days were fraught with challenges. Schweitzer and his wife initially operated out of a former chicken hut, dealing with a multitude of tropical diseases and injuries, often with limited resources. Yet, they persevered. Within nine months, they treated around 2,000 patients, many of whom traveled great distances for the chance of healing. Schweitzer's dedication to serving others was unyielding, reflecting his belief that our dreams must extend beyond ourselves to touch the lives of those in need.

Perseverance in Adversity: Service Through Trials

Even in the face of adversity, Schweitzer's commitment to his dream never wavered. During World War I, as German nationals in a French colony, Schweitzer and his wife were interned. Yet rather than see this as a setback, Schweitzer used the time to recover from illness and reflect on his mission. He emerged with a renewed sense of purpose, focused on continuing his work in Africa.

A Legacy of Service: Sowing Seeds for the Future

Throughout his life, Albert Schweitzer exemplified the idea that our dreams are not truly ours—they are seeds sown for the benefit of others. His work in Lambaréné extended beyond providing immediate medical care; it was about creating a sustainable healthcare environment that could continue to serve the community long after he was gone. Schweitzer's dream was rooted in a deep commitment to service, a dream that continues to inspire generations to live beyond themselves.

"Life becomes harder for us when we live for others, but it also becomes richer and happier," Schweitzer once reflected. This wisdom captures the essence of living a dream that serves others. By dedicating his life to the well-being of humanity, Schweitzer found a deeper sense of purpose and fulfillment. His story teaches us that while the path of service may be challenging, it is infinitely rewarding, both for ourselves and for those we seek to help.

Living Your Dream for Humanity

Albert Schweitzer's life is a powerful reminder that our dreams are not solely about our own ambitions or successes. They are about the lasting impact we can have on the world and the lives we touch along the way. Schweitzer's unwavering dedication to serving others, even at great personal cost, exemplifies the ultimate fulfillment that comes from living a dream for the benefit of humanity. His legacy encourages us all to ask ourselves: How can our dreams make a difference? And in what ways can we, like Schweitzer, sow seeds today that will benefit others tomorrow?

"The purpose of human life is to serve, and to show compassion and the will to help others." Let this be the guiding light for our dreams, as it was for Albert Schweitzer, reminding us that the true fulfillment of our aspirations lies not in what we achieve for ourselves, but in what we contribute to the lives of others.

The True Measure of Success: Beyond Personal Ambitions

"Success is knowing your purpose in life, sowing seeds that benefit others, and growing to your maximum potential," says Dr. John Maxwell, a mentor and renowned leadership expert. He believes success isn't reserved for a select few but is attainable by everyone. The secret? It lies in your daily habits, rooted in your dreams, vision, and unwavering self-discipline.

Dr. John Maxwell emphasizes that success isn't just about achieving personal milestones. "When you know your purpose in life and are growing to reach your maximum potential, you're well on your way to being a success. But there's one more important part to the success journey: helping others. Without that aspect, the journey can be a lonely and shallow experience."

Success is Not About Us—It's About Impacting Others

It's often said that we make a living by what we get, but we make a life by what we give. This sentiment is echoed in the powerful words of Albert Schweitzer, an Austria-born physician and humanitarian who declared, "The purpose of human life is to serve, and to show compassion and the will to help others." His journey took him to Africa, where he devoted many years to serving others. For him, success was about far more than personal gain; it was about making a meaningful difference in the lives of others.

For most of us, sowing seeds that benefit others doesn't require moving across the globe. You don't have to embark on a mission to a distant country to find your purpose—unless, of course, that is your calling. If that's the case, you won't find satisfaction until you're fulfilling that mission. That is what happened to me sixteen years ago when I left the nation where I was born for the United States, not for greener pasture according to popular thinking but to fulfill my mission on earth. But for many, helping others begins right where we are, in the everyday moments that define our lives.

The Power of Serving in Your Own Backyard

Helping others might mean spending quality time with your family, mentoring an employee who shows great promise, or contributing to your local community. It could even be as simple as putting your personal desires on hold for the benefit of your team at work. The crucial thing is to recognize that our dreams are not just about us—they're about making a difference in the lives of those around us.

Dreams Fulfilled Through Service

As entertainer Danny Thomas once said, "All of us are born for a reason, but all of us don't discover why. Success in life has nothing to do with what you gain in life or accomplish for yourself. It's what you do for others." Success isn't measured by our own achievements but by the positive impact we have on others.

So, as you pursue your dreams, remember this: **Your dreams are not just about you—they're about what you can do for others.** When you live with that mindset, you don't just achieve success; you inspire it in others, creating a ripple effect that can change the world. One of my favorite quotes is by an American author and disability rights advocate, Helen Keller: "Life is an exciting business, and most exciting when it is lived for others." This quote has shaped my life and leadership over the years, making me live my dream and experience true fulfillment through serving the needs of others. Author, speaker and coach, Tony Robbins said, "Only those who have learned the power of sincere and selfless contribution experience life's deepest joy: true fulfillment."

Self-Activity for *Chapter Five*

Reflect on these thought-provoking questions to explore how your dream can positively impact others. This will help shift your focus from personal achievement to meaningful contribution.

1. **Who Will Benefit from Your Dream?**
   Think about the people who will be impacted by your dream. How will their lives improve because you pursued it?

2. **What Problem Does Your Dream Solve?**
   Every dream has the potential to address a need. What problem or challenge does your dream aim to solve for others?

3. **How Can You Serve Others Through Your Dream Today?**
   What actions can you take right now to begin serving others with your dream, even in a small way?

4. **What Legacy Do You Want to Leave?**
   Consider the long-term impact of your dream. How can it leave a legacy that benefits future generations?

5. **Who Can You Inspire Along the Way?**
   As you live your dream, who might you inspire or encourage to pursue their own? How can you help others do the same?

Use these questions to guide your actions and ensure your dream contributes to a greater purpose—making a difference in the lives of others!

CHAPTER SIX
PRACTICAL BLUEPRINT FOR LIVING LIFE BIG!

"The only tragedy greater than dying with dreams unfulfilled is never to have dreamed at all." – John Maxwell.

A blueprint, in its simplest form, is a detailed plan or guide that outlines the steps needed to achieve a specific goal. Just as architects rely on blueprints to construct buildings with precision, leaders and organizations use blueprints to build successful projects, strategies, and futures. A blueprint isn't just about the "what" but the "how"—it lays out the essential elements, the sequence of actions, and the expected outcomes.

The Power of a Blueprint

The power of a blueprint lies in its ability to transform vision into reality. It provides clarity and direction, ensuring that everyone involved understands their roles and responsibilities. With a blueprint, the risks of deviation and ambiguity are minimized, allowing for a more focused and streamlined approach.

1. **Clarity and Focus**: A well-defined blueprint provides a clear picture of the desired outcome, and the steps required to get there. It reduces uncertainty and allows for a more concentrated effort toward the goal.

2. **Efficiency and Resource Management**: By mapping out every step and resource required, a blueprint helps in managing time, money, and manpower more effectively. This ensures that resources are used optimally, minimizing waste and maximizing productivity.

3. **Risk Management**: Having a blueprint allows you to foresee potential challenges and plan for them in advance. This proactive approach to risk management reduces the likelihood of unexpected setbacks, ensuring smoother execution.

4. **Consistency and Alignment**: A blueprint ensures that everyone is on the same page, promoting consistency in action and decision-making. It aligns the team's efforts with the organization's goals, leading to cohesive progress toward the desired outcome.

5. **Flexibility within Structure**: While a blueprint provides a structured approach, it also allows for flexibility. Should circumstances change, a good blueprint can be adjusted to accommodate new information or unexpected challenges without losing sight of the end goal.

The Benefits of Having an Effective and Practical Blueprint

An effective blueprint is not just detailed but also practical. It considers real-world variables and constraints, making it a realistic guide that can be followed.

1. **Guides Strategic Decision-Making**: An effective blueprint lays the groundwork for making informed decisions. It serves as a reference point, helping leaders weigh options against the long-term vision and objectives of the organization.

2. **Enhances Communication**: With a clear blueprint, communication within a team or organization becomes more straightforward. Everyone knows what the end goal is and how their contributions fit into the bigger picture.

3. **Improves Accountability**: When roles, responsibilities, and deadlines are clearly defined, it is easier to hold people accountable. A blueprint ensures that each team member knows what is expected of them and when, fostering a culture of responsibility.

4. **Encourages Innovation within Constraints**: While a blueprint provides structure, it also encourages creativity and innovation. By setting boundaries, it challenges individuals and teams to think creatively within those limits to find the best possible solutions.

5. **Facilitates Achievement of Goals**: Ultimately, a blueprint helps in achieving goals more effectively. By providing a clear path from start to finish, it enables the efficient accomplishment of objectives, driving success and growth.

A True Story: The Power of a Blueprint in Action

To illustrate the power and benefits of having a blueprint, consider the story of Tirtha Chavan, a global business transformation leader at Salesforce. Tirtha has been instrumental in driving profitable growth, customer outcomes, and operational efficiency across the organization. Her success is rooted in the meticulous planning and execution of business transformation strategies.

Tirtha emphasizes the importance of setting SMART goals—Specific, Measurable, Achievable, Relevant, and Time-bound—as the foundation of any effective blueprint. She believes that successful business transformation begins with clear, well-defined SMART goals that serve as a compass for all subsequent actions.

In one of her notable projects at Salesforce, Tirtha was tasked with leading a major transformation initiative aimed at increasing operational efficiency while driving customer satisfaction. The challenge was immense, involving multiple teams across different continents, each with its own unique set of challenges and priorities.

To navigate this complexity, Tirtha developed a comprehensive blueprint. She began by conducting thorough market and internal analyses to identify opportunities and threats. This initial phase was crucial, as it provided the data-driven insights needed to set realistic and impactful SMART goals.

With these goals in place, Tirtha laid out a step-by-step plan that outlined the specific actions required, the resources needed, and the timelines for completion. This blueprint became the guiding document for the entire initiative, ensuring that every team member, regardless of location, was aligned with the overall objectives.

The result? Not only did the initiative achieve its primary goals of increasing efficiency and enhancing customer satisfaction, but it also fostered a culture of collaboration and innovation within the company. Teams were more aligned, communication was more effective, and everyone had a clear understanding of their roles and responsibilities.

This success story underscores the importance of having a well-defined and practical blueprint. It shows how a structured, yet flexible plan can guide an organization through complex challenges, ensuring that everyone is moving in the same direction and working towards the same end goal.

A blueprint therefore is more than just a plan—it's a powerful tool that can transform vision into reality. It provides the clarity, direction, and structure needed to navigate the complexities of any project or initiative. Whether you're leading a team, managing a project, or driving organizational change, having an effective and practical blueprint is essential for success.

Practical Blueprint for Living Life Big: The DREAM Acronym Revealed!

To live your dream, you need more than just passion—you need a plan. The DREAM acronym is not just a set of words; it's a comprehensive blueprint for success. It combines vision (Dream Factor), perseverance (Resilience Factor), collaboration (Embrace Teamwork Factor), commitment (Accountability Partnership Factor), and wisdom (Mentorship Factor) to create a powerful framework for LIVING LIFE BIG.

The DREAM Acronym: Your Blueprint for Living Life Big

As you embark on the journey to live life big, remember the powerful acronym DREAM:

- **D**ream Factor
- **R**esilience Factor
- **E**mbrace Teamwork Factor
- **A**ccountability Partnership Factor
- **M**entorship Factor

The DREAM acronym helps you stay aligned with your passions and purpose, ensuring that you don't just leave your dreams behind but actively live them out each day.

Live Life BIG: The Power of a Dream-Driven Life

When you live life according to your dreams, you experience a sense of fulfillment and purpose that's unmatched. You wake up every day excited about what's possible, not afraid of what might go wrong. *"The future belongs to those who believe in the beauty of their dreams,"* said Eleanor Roosevelt. Your dream is your unique blueprint for greatness, and by following the

DREAM acronym, you position yourself to not just achieve but to excel beyond your wildest expectations.

A GLIMPSE INTO THE DREAM ACRONYM

"Dying is nothing. What is terrible is not to live." – Victor Hugo.

Dream Factor - Ignite the Spark: Dream Big, Start Small, Act Now!

Dreams are the fire that fuels our passion and purpose. They are the visions that pull us towards a future that feels both exciting and significant. But dreaming is more than just imagining what could be—it's about taking actionable steps to make those dreams a reality. As Walt Disney said, *"All our dreams can come true if we have the courage to pursue them."* Ignite the power of your dreams by daring to dream big, starting small, and acting now. Your dream is the blueprint for a life lived fully and authentically.

Resilience Factor: Bounce Back, Rise Higher

Life will throw curveballs, and there will be moments when you feel like giving up. But remember, it's not about how many times you fall—it's about how many times you rise. Resilience is the secret sauce to turning setbacks into comebacks. Oprah Winfrey once said, *"Turn your wounds into wisdom."* Every challenge is an opportunity to learn, grow, and come back stronger. Embrace the resilience factor and watch as you transform obstacles into steppingstones toward your dreams.

Embrace Teamwork Factor: Together We Achieve More

No one succeeds alone. Great achievements are often the result of collaboration and synergy. *"Alone we can do so little; together we can do so much,"* said Helen Keller. By embracing teamwork, you tap into a pool of diverse talents, ideas, and strengths that elevate everyone involved. Understand the power of collaboration and how it accelerates the journey to living your dream. When we work together, our collective energy can move mountains and make the impossible possible.

Accountability Partnership Factor: Stay on Track, Stay Committed

It's easy to drift off course when the path gets tough. That's where an accountability partnership comes in. It's a mutual commitment to stay focused on your goals and push each other to achieve more. *"Accountability is the glue that ties commitment to the result,"* says Bob Proctor. Find someone who believes in your dream as much as you do and can hold you accountable. Together, you'll build the discipline needed to stay on track and achieve your dreams.

Mentorship Factor: Learn from Those Who've Walked the Path

Mentorship is like having a personal GPS for your journey. It offers guidance, support, and the benefit of experience. Tony Robbins once said, *"A real decision is measured by the fact that you've taken a new action. If there's no action, you haven't truly decided."* A mentor helps you take those decisive steps, offering insights and advice from their own experiences. By learning from those who have walked the path, you can avoid common pitfalls and fast-track your way to success.

Your Dreams Are Worth the Journey

"Fear does not prevent death. It prevents life." – Naguib Mahfouz (Egyptian Author and 1988 Nobel Peace Winner in Literature).

Living your dream is the ultimate adventure. It's a journey filled with highs and lows, challenges and triumphs. But remember, the pursuit of your dream is worth every step. As you apply the principles in this chapter, you'll discover that the power to live life BIG is already within you. So, ignite your dream, build your resilience, embrace teamwork, find your accountability partner, and learn from mentors. Your dream is calling—are you ready to answer?

This chapter is your invitation to not just leave your dreams on the drawing board but to bring them to life. So, get ready to embark on the most exciting journey of all—the journey of living your dream!

Self-Activity for *Chapter Six*

Use these questions to help create your own practical blueprint for living your dream. They will guide you toward clarity, action, and alignment with your purpose.

1. **What's Your Vision?**
   What is the one dream or goal you want to achieve that will define living life BIG for you? Be specific.

2. **What Steps Can You Take Right Now?**
   Break your dream into smaller steps. What is the first actionable step you can take today to move closer to your dream?

3. **What Challenges Might You Face?**
   Consider the obstacles that could stand in your way. How can you proactively plan to overcome them?

4. **Who Can You Collaborate With?**
   Identify the people or resources that can help you achieve your dream. Who can you team up with for support or accountability?

5. **What's Your Timeline?**
   Set a specific, time-bound goal. When do you want to achieve your dream, and what milestones will you set along the way?

Reflect on these questions, and use your answers to craft a personalized, practical blueprint that will help you live your dream and *live life BIG!*

CHAPTER SEVEN
DREAM FACTOR

"All our dreams can come if we have the courage to pursue them." – Walt Disney.

D – Dream Factor: The Seed of Possibility

Everything starts with a dream. The journey to greatness often begins with a single, powerful vision. But a dream alone is not enough; it requires resilience, teamwork, accountability, and mentorship to transform that vision into reality.

Walt Disney once said, "If you can dream it, you can do it." Allow yourself to dream big and visualize a future that excites and inspires you. Your dream is the blueprint for your journey—it's the vision that will guide you through life's challenges and triumphs.

A dream worth pursuing is a predictor and blueprint of a person's purpose and potential. But what exactly is a dream? Sharon Hull defined a dream as, "The seed of possibility planted in the soul of a human being, which calls him to pursue a unique path to the realization of his purpose." The phrase "seed of possibility" stands out as a reminder of the transformative power of a true dream when it is planted in the soul of a human being.

Consider Dr. Martin Luther King Jr., whose dream of equality and justice for all sparked the Civil Rights Movement in the United States. His famous "I Have a Dream" speech, delivered during the March on

Washington for Jobs and Freedom on August 28, 1963, was a catalyst for change. It was more than just a speech; it was a call to action that resonated with millions, leading to monumental shifts in society. When you live your dream, you don't just change your life—you can change the world.

Imagine living a life where every morning you wake up energized, fueled by a vision so compelling that it pulls you out of bed with excitement. Now, contrast that with a life lived in mediocrity, where dreams are buried under the weight of routine and fear. The renowned American comedian John Florence Sullivan, known professionally as Fred Allen, once remarked, "You only live once. But if you work it right, once is enough." If we truly only live once, why not make that life extraordinary? Why settle for small when you can live big? Why embrace the status quo when you can reach for the stars and become the best version of yourself for the benefit of humanity?

These are not just rhetorical questions; they are a call to action, an invitation to step into a life of purpose and passion. This chapter is dedicated to exploring the transformative power of a dream—the Dream Factor—in living a life that is not just big, but monumental.

The Power of a Dream: More Than Just Wishful Thinking

Living life big is not an automatic process. If wishes were horses, all beggars would ride. It requires more than just desire; it demands intentionality, commitment, and action. To *LIVE LIFE BIG*, you must not LEAVE your dream behind—you must LIVE your dream! Every person who has ever achieved greatness shares one common trait: a dream they believed in with unwavering conviction. They channeled the energy from that dream into their will, emotions, and mind, empowering them to do everything within their power to bring it to fruition.

Walt Disney: The Dreamer Who Built a Kingdom

Walt Disney embodies the essence of living life big through the power of a dream. He famously said, "All our dreams can come true, if we have the courage to pursue them." Disney's dream started with a simple cartoon character and grew into a global entertainment empire. Despite numerous setbacks and financial challenges, his unwavering vision and determination made Disneyland and Disney World a reality—places where dreams come alive every day. Disney didn't just have a dream; he lived it, breathed it, and turned it into a legacy that continues to inspire millions.

Sam Walton: Revolutionizing Retail with a Dream

Another inspiring example is Sam Walton, the founder of Walmart. Walton didn't leave his dream behind; he lived it to the fullest. He believed in providing customers with affordable goods and revolutionized the retail industry with his innovative practices. His mantra, "High expectations are the key to everything," propelled Walmart to become the world's largest retailer. Walton's dream was not just about building a business; it was about changing the way people shopped, making quality products accessible to everyone. His grand expectations for himself and his company transformed the retail landscape forever.

The Persistence of Purpose: Don't Watch the Clock, Keep Going

American humorist and author Sam Levenson once said, "Don't watch the clock; do what it does. Keep going." This quote is a powerful reminder that persistence and determination are essential in the pursuit of our dreams. Time waits for no one, but those who persist in the face of challenges are the ones who see their dreams come to life. Living your dream requires more than just vision—it requires the resilience to keep going, even when the path is steep, and the journey is long.

Living the Dream: From Vision to Reality

When you leave your dream and don't live it, you deny yourself the opportunity to live life big. Abandoning your dream dims your world, while living your dream brightens your universe! As my mentor, Dr. John Maxwell, defines it: "A dream is an inspiring picture of the future that energizes your mind, will, and emotions, empowering you to do everything you can to achieve it." This is why everyone must find their dream and live it to experience true fulfillment and to live life on a grand scale.

Your Call to Action: Live Your Dream, Don't Leave It

Remember this: To truly *LIVE LIFE BIG*, you must live your dream, not leave it. Every great achievement in history started as a dream in someone's mind. Your dream is your compass, your guide, and your source of strength. Embrace it, nurture it, and let it propel you to heights you've never imagined.

Live life big by living your dream—and watch as your dream transforms not just your life, but the lives of those around you.

Self-Activity for Chapter Seven

Reflect on these questions to awaken the "seed of possibility" within you and activate the power of your dream. This will help you turn your dream into a driving force for your life.

1. **What Is Your Dream?**
   Think of a dream that excites and energizes you. What vision do you have for your life that makes you feel alive and driven?

2. **Why Is This Dream Important?**
   Explore why this dream matters to you. How does it align with your purpose and values?

3. **What Is Holding You Back?**
   Identify the fears, doubts, or obstacles that might be keeping you from pursuing your dream fully. How can you overcome them?

4. **What Small Step Can You Take Today?**
   Dreams start with action. What practical step can you take today to move closer to living your dream?

5. **Who Can Support You on This Journey?**
   Think about who can provide encouragement, accountability, or mentorship as you pursue your dream. Who can help you stay committed?

Use these questions to spark clarity, passion, and purpose, and start living your dream!

CHAPTER EIGHT: RESILIENCE FACTOR

"Persistence and resilience only come from having been given the chance to work through difficult problems." – Gever Tulley.

In the last chapter, we delved into the **Dream Factor** of the DREAM acronym, the driving force behind living life big. Now, let's explore the **Resilience Factor**, the second critical element of the acronym, essential for turning dreams into reality.

Resilience: The Unbreakable Spirit

Resilience is the ability to withstand, adapt, and thrive despite adversity. It's the unbreakable spirit that propels us forward when the world pushes us down. Without resilience, dreams remain fragile; with it, they become indestructible. Imagine resilience as the glue that holds your dreams together through the storms of life, ensuring they don't just survive but flourish.

The PURPOSE Acronym: A Roadmap to Resilience

To cultivate resilience, embody the principles of the **PURPOSE** acronym. This roadmap will guide you through life's challenges and help you maintain the strength to keep pursuing your dreams.

- **P = Picture Your Possibilities**
  Visualizing success is the first step in building resilience. Helen Keller said, "Optimism is the faith that leads to achievement. Nothing can be done

without hope and confidence." By picturing your possibilities, you fuel the resilience needed to overcome obstacles and keep moving toward your dream.

- **U = Use Failure as a Learning Tool**
  Failure is not the end but a crucial step toward success. Thomas Edison's famous words, "I have not failed. I've just found 10,000 ways that won't work," remind us that each failure teaches us something valuable. Embrace these lessons as the foundation for resilience, turning setbacks into setups for your comeback.

- **R = Reach Out for Support**
  No one succeeds alone. Brene Brown said, "We don't have to do all of it alone. We were never meant to." Seeking support from others, whether friends, family, or mentors, provides the encouragement and perspective necessary to stay resilient.

- **P = Put Things in the Right Perspective**
  Perspective shapes resilience. Anais Nin's insight, "We don't see things as they are, we see them as we are," highlights the importance of reframing challenges. By viewing difficulties as opportunities for growth, you can maintain the mental clarity needed to stay resilient.

- **O = Operate with Optimism**
  Winston Churchill wisely noted, "The pessimist sees difficulty in every opportunity. The optimist sees opportunity in every difficulty." Optimism

isn't just about seeing the bright side; it's about believing in your ability to overcome challenges and achieve your dreams.

- **S = Serve Others**
  Service strengthens resilience. Mahatma Gandhi's words, "The best way to find yourself is to lose yourself in the service of others," remind us that contributing to something larger than ourselves can anchor us during difficult times. Serving others not only builds resilience but also enriches your life with purpose and meaning.

- **E = Embrace Joy**
  Joy is a powerful antidote to adversity. Henri Nouwen said, "Joy does not simply happen to us. We have to choose joy and keep choosing it every day." By focusing on what brings you happiness, you build the emotional resilience needed to persevere through challenges.

These are not just rhetorical questions; they are a call to action, an invitation to step into a life of purpose and passion. This chapter is dedicated to exploring the transformative power of resilience—Resilience Factor—in living a life that is not just big, but monumental.

Historical Inspiration: Abraham Lincoln's Journey

"Always bear in mind that your own resolution to succeed is more important than any other." – Abraham Lincoln.

Abraham Lincoln's story is one of remarkable resilience. From his humble beginnings to becoming the 16th President of the United States, Lincoln faced numerous setbacks, including business failures, election defeats, and personal tragedies. Yet, his unwavering resolve and resilience not only led him to greatness but also to the preservation of the United States during its darkest hour.

Imagine if Lincoln had abandoned his dream after facing so many obstacles. The world would have lost a leader whose legacy continues to inspire generations. Lincoln's resilience turned potential failures into triumphs, proving that setbacks are merely setups for greater success.

Resilience in Action: Living Your Dream

When we abandon our dreams, we deprive the world of what could have been. Resilience is the key to keeping those dreams alive and ensuring they don't just remain fantasies but become realities that impact the world.

Resilience is not just a trait; it's a choice. Choose to be resilient. Choose to keep going, no matter the obstacles. By doing so, you'll live your dream and, in turn, live life big.

My Resilience Story: From Setbacks to Comebacks!

Exactly 29 years ago, I embarked on a journey that would test my resilience in ways I never imagined. I gained admission to one of the most prestigious colleges in West Africa, the University of Ibadan, Nigeria to study medicine and surgery. This achievement was the culmination of five years of relentless pursuit, during which I faced numerous setbacks, including failing the entrance examination three times before finally succeeding on my fourth attempt in 1994 and gaining the admission in 1995.

The Early Struggles: A Wake-Up Call

Entering this highly coveted institution was a dream come true, but my initial approach to my studies was far from ideal. As a freshman, I lacked the discipline necessary for such a rigorous program. I believed I could scrape by with last-minute cramming, a habit that carried me through the early stages of my education. However, when I reached the pre-clinical school, where subjects like Anatomy, Biochemistry, and Physiology required long-term consistency instead of short-term intensity, my shortcomings became painfully evident.

I failed my first professional exam, a crushing blow that meant repeating the class and watching my former classmates advance without me. This was a defining moment—a test of my resilience. But instead of letting this setback defeat me, I chose to learn from it. I adopted a new philosophy: "Long-term consistency trumps short-term intensity." This shift in mindset, coupled with new habits and a renewed focus, transformed my approach to studying. I was so consistent that one of my colleagues began calling me "Consistency." Through sheer determination, I passed the exam with good grades and moved on to the clinical phase of my medical training.

The Final Hurdles: Resilience Refined

As I approached the end of my medical training, I encountered challenges even more daunting than those I faced earlier. These setbacks tested my resilience on a deeper level. I remember nights spent sleeping on hard tables and chairs in remote locations, sacrificing comfort and leisure for the sake of my dream. I was determined to see it through, no matter the cost.

American actor Robert Strauss once said, "Success is a little like wrestling a gorilla. You don't quit when you're tired—you quit when the gorilla is tired." This quote encapsulates the essence of resilience. It's about pushing through exhaustion, frustration, and doubt until you've overcome the obstacles in your path. As Winston Churchill famously said, "Never, never, never give up." Each setback was not an end but a setup for a greater comeback.

The Resilience Factor: Lessons Learned

Through this journey, I learned that resilience is not just about bouncing back—it's about growing stronger with each challenge. It's about understanding that setbacks are an inevitable part of the process and that each one presents an opportunity to refine your character, sharpen your focus, and strengthen your resolve.

"The Power of Persistence: Wrestling with Your Gorilla"

Resilience is the force that propels you forward when everything else is pushing you back. It's the quiet strength that refuses to quit, the unwavering belief that your dream is worth the struggle. My story is a testament to the fact that resilience, when paired with a clear vision and unyielding determination, can turn any setback into a powerful comeback.

So, if you find yourself facing challenges that seem insurmountable, remember this: Success isn't about avoiding difficulties—it's about persisting through them.

Your dream is within reach, and with resilience as your guide, you can live life big by living your dream, not leaving it behind.

Self-Activity for Chapter Eight

Reflect on these questions to strengthen your resilience and empower yourself to turn setbacks into comebacks. This will help you stay determined and keep moving toward your dreams.

1. **What Challenges Have You Overcome?**
   Think of a significant setback you've faced. How did you overcome it, and what did you learn from the experience?

2. **How Do You Handle Failure?**
   When you face failure or disappointment, how do you react? What can you change in your mindset or approach to turn failure into a learning opportunity?

3. **Who Can Support You?**
   Who are the people you can turn to for support and encouragement during tough times? How can you lean on them to help you stay resilient?

4. **What's Your Long-Term Goal?**
   Revisit your ultimate dream or goal. How does keeping your eye on this big picture help you push through difficult moments?

5. **What Small Step Can You Take Today to Build Resilience?**
   Resilience is built through action. What small, consistent step can you take today to strengthen your resilience and move closer to your dream?

Use these questions to embrace resilience, knowing that every challenge is an opportunity to grow stronger and closer to achieving your dream!

CHAPTER NINE
EMBRACE TEAMWORK FACTOR

"A successful team is a group of many hands and one mind." – Bill Bethel.

The Power of "We" Over "Me"

"Alone we can do so little; together we can do so much." — Helen Keller.

In the pursuit of living life big and turning dreams into reality, embracing teamwork stands as a cornerstone principle. The journey toward achieving monumental goals is rarely a solo endeavor; it thrives on the collective strength, wisdom, and synergy of a dedicated team. This chapter delves into the essence of teamwork, exploring how uniting with others amplifies our abilities, accelerates our progress, and enriches our experiences.

The Essence of Teamwork: Beyond Individual Effort

"If you want to go fast, go alone. If you want to go far, go together." — African Proverb.

Teamwork is more than just working alongside others; it's about merging diverse talents, perspectives, and energies toward a common purpose. It's the understanding that while individual efforts are important, collective collaboration can achieve the extraordinary. When we embrace teamwork, we open ourselves to learning, growth, and possibilities that exceed our singular capabilities.

My Journey with the Maxwell Leadership Team: A Transformation Through Collaboration

"Coming together is a beginning. Keeping together is progress. Working together is success." — Henry Ford.

In May 2020, I embarked on a transformative journey by joining the Maxwell Leadership Team, and my life has never been the same since. Led by my mentor, Dr. John Maxwell—hailed as the world's foremost leadership guru and a prolific author on leadership—the team embodies the true spirit of collaborative growth and excellence.

With over fifty-four dynamic and high-caliber Coaches, the Maxwell Leadership Team provides a nurturing and empowering environment that fosters personal and professional development. This global community is a testament to the profound impact of teamwork:

- **Shared Wisdom:** Learning from seasoned leaders and diverse minds has broadened my horizons and deepened my understanding of effective leadership.

- **Supportive Network:** The camaraderie and mutual support within the team have been instrumental in overcoming challenges and celebrating successes.

- **Collective Impact:** Together, we've influenced countless lives worldwide, demonstrating that united efforts can drive significant, positive change.

As Dr. John Maxwell humorously puts it, *"If you want to climb a little hill, you don't need a team, just a pair of sneakers. But if you want to climb Mount Everest, you need a team because as the challenges escalate, teamwork will elevate."* This analogy beautifully captures the indispensable role of teamwork in achieving lofty and impactful dreams.

Building the LAMP Global Community: Unity in Action!

"Talent wins games, but teamwork and intelligence win championships." — Michael Jordan.

Fueled by the inspiration and lessons from the Maxwell Leadership Team, I founded the **LAMP Global Community** nineteen months ago with a vision for global transformation. What started as a dream has blossomed into a vibrant community of twenty-one dedicated leaders united by shared values and a positive attitude.

Our Collective Accomplishments:

- **Leadership Masterclasses:** We've conducted numerous virtual masterclasses that have empowered individuals from different nations to discover and hone their leadership potential.

- **Global Leadership Conferences:** Hosting five virtual global conferences focused on leadership for men, women, parents, and youth, we've touched and transformed lives across continents.

- **Upcoming Endeavors:** We are currently gearing up for the **MADE FOR MORE GLOBAL LEADERSHIP CONFERENCE 4.0** with six seasoned and experienced speakers next March 1, 2025, themed *"Unveiling the Essence of Servant Leadership."* This event aims to inspire attendees to transcend personal achievements and contribute meaningfully to the world.

These accomplishments underscore the profound truth that **"Teamwork makes the dream work."** By pooling our strengths, resources, and passions, we've created ripples of positive change that continue to expand globally.

The TEAM Acronym: Together Everyone Achieves More

"None of us is as smart as all of us." — Ken Blanchard.

The word **TEAM** itself encapsulates the magic of collaboration:

- **T – Together**
- **E – Everyone**
- **A – Achieves**
- **M – More**

This simple yet powerful acronym reminds us that our collective efforts can lead to results far greater than what we could achieve individually. It's through unity and cooperation that dreams are not only realized but also amplified.

Andrew Carnegie, the renowned industrialist and philanthropist, aptly stated, *"Teamwork is the ability to work together toward a common vision. The ability to direct individual accomplishments toward organizational objectives. It is the fuel that allows common people to attain uncommon results."* This insight emphasizes that greatness is attainable when we align our individual talents and efforts toward a shared goal.

Surrounding Yourself with the Right Team: Choosing Your Dream Builders

"Find a group of people who challenge and inspire you, spend a lot of time with them, and it will change your life forever." — Amy Poehler.

Choosing the right team is crucial in the journey toward living life big:

- **Shared Vision:** Aligning with individuals who understand and are passionate about your dream creates a cohesive and motivated unit.

- **Diverse Skills:** A team with varied skills and expertise brings comprehensive solutions and innovative ideas to the table.

- **Positive Attitude:** Optimism and resilience within the team foster a supportive and encouraging environment that propels everyone forward.

Mattie J.T. Stepanek, a young but profound poet and peace advocate, wisely said, *"Unity is strength... when there is teamwork and collaboration, wonderful things can be achieved."* Surrounding yourself with a team that embodies unity, and collaboration turns monumental dreams into achievable realities.

Embracing Teamwork: Steps to Building and Sustaining Effective Teams

"The strength of the team is each individual member. The strength of each member is the team." — Phil Jackson.

To fully embrace teamwork, consider the following steps:

1. **Define a Clear Purpose:** Ensure that all team members understand and are committed to the overarching goal.

2. **Foster Open Communication:** Create an environment where ideas and feedback are freely exchanged and valued.

3. **Encourage Mutual Respect:** Recognize and appreciate the unique contributions of each team member.

4. **Promote Collaboration:** Encourage working together on tasks and projects, leveraging collective strengths.

5. **Resolve Conflicts Constructively:** Address disagreements promptly and fairly, turning challenges into growth opportunities.

6. **Celebrate Achievements Together:** Acknowledge and celebrate both individual and team successes to build morale and cohesion.

By implementing these principles, you cultivate a team that is not only effective but also fulfilling to be a part of.

The Height of Your Dream is Limited by the Strength of Your Team!

"Great things in business are never done by one person; they're done by a team of people." — Steve Jobs.

Living life big and actualizing your dreams is a journey enriched and empowered by embracing teamwork. Through collective effort, shared vision, and mutual support, what once seemed impossible becomes attainable. Remember, **you can't do life big alone; you need the right team with the same dream.**

As you pursue your aspirations, seek out those who will climb alongside you, contribute their strengths, and share in the triumphs and lessons along the way. Together, you will not only reach your goals but also create lasting impact and meaningful change in the world.

"Coming together is a beginning; keeping together is progress; working together is success." — Henry Ford.

Embrace teamwork, live your dream, and watch as you and your team achieve more than you ever thought possible.

Self-Activity for Chapter Nine

Reflect on these questions to explore how embracing teamwork can elevate your dream and lead to greater success. Use them to inspire collaboration and build a strong, effective team.

1. **Who Is on Your Team?**
   Think about the people who are already helping you pursue your dream. Are they the right fit? Who else could you invite to join your team to enhance its strength?

2. **What Skills Are Missing?**
   Consider the skills, knowledge, or perspectives your team might be lacking. How can you bring in people who fill those gaps and complement your strengths?

3. **How Well Are You Collaborating?**
   Evaluate the level of collaboration within your team. Are there opportunities for better communication or shared decision-making?

4. **What Is Your Team's Common Purpose?**
   Identify the shared vision that unites your team. How can you reinforce that purpose to keep everyone aligned and motivated?

5. **How Can You Celebrate Success Together?**
   Reflect on how you can acknowledge and celebrate your team's collective achievements. What can you do to build morale and foster a sense of accomplishment?

Use these questions to build a strong, motivated team and embrace the power of working together toward your dream!

CHAPTER TEN
ACCOUNTABILITY PARTNERSHIP FACTOR: YOUR BRIDGE FROM INTENTION TO REALITY

"Accountability is the glue that ties commitment to the result." – Bob Proctor.

A - Accountability Partnership Factor: The Catalyst for Transformation

"Accountability breeds response-ability." — Stephen Covey.

In the pursuit of our dreams, there is often a gap between what we intend to do and what we accomplish. Accountability serves as the bridge between intention and reality. As Dr. John Maxwell wisely states, "The greatest way to improve your life is to be accountable to someone. Accountability closes the gap between intention and result." Without accountability, intentions remain mere wishes; it is the consistent check-in with others that turns these wishes into results.

The Power of Intentional Accountability

Accountability is not passive; it requires intentionality. It demands a commitment to not just *meaning* well but *doing* well. My personal journey is a testament to this truth. Through various accountability partnerships, I've seen my intentions transform into tangible results. I've learned that you can't **amount** to anything when you don't **account** for your actions.

For example, my accountability partnerships in daily reading, personal growth, and leadership development have been pivotal. I've committed to reporting back to my group with each new book I complete, and this simple act of accountability has kept me consistent and driven.

TRAIN: Igniting Passion, Unlocking Potential, and Fostering Connection!

In late 2023, I founded TRAIN: The Reading Addict Inspired Nation, with a three-point agenda:

1. **Ignite Imagination**: Books open doors to unexplored worlds, untapped ideas, and unleashed dreams. They allow you to immerse yourself in magic that only reading can provide.

2. **Unleash Potential**: Reading is more than a habit; it's a catalyst for personal growth. By embracing reading, you unlock your true potential and discover the extraordinary within you.

3. **Connect with Like Minds**: TRAIN is a community of passionate individuals who share a love for the written word. We discuss, share, and connect with like-minded souls on a journey of self-discovery.

As a result of this accountability-driven community, I now read from nine different books every day (I don't finish the nine books but consistently read from them daily), intentionally investing in my own personal growth. This relentless commitment to growth today is an investment in the opportunities of tomorrow.

The LAMP Global Community Authors' Forum: Accountability in Action

Through the LAMP Global Community, I launched an authors' forum four months ago to ensure accountability in my book writing journey. This forum has become a thriving space for both seasoned and prospective authors, where we meet monthly to review our progress, encourage one another, and stay focused on our goal of publishing our books. Thanks to this accountability partnership, I am now working on my tenth book (this book in your hand).

The Power of PEER: Positive, Enriching, Encouraging Relationships

To fully embrace the accountability partnership factor, it is essential to surround yourself with the right people—those who will hold you accountable, motivate you, and share in your journey. I like to refer to this as the power of PEER:

- **P - Positive**: Surround yourself with individuals who bring positivity and optimism into your life.

- **E - Enriching**: Choose partners who enrich your journey with wisdom, knowledge, and valuable insights.

- **E - Encouraging**: A great accountability partner encourages you during both the highs and the lows.

- **R - Relationships**: Build strong relationships founded on mutual respect, trust, and a shared vision.

John Di Lemme once said, "Accountability separates the wishers in life from the action-takers that care enough about their future to account for their daily actions." This speaks to the heart of accountability—it's the difference between those who LEAVE their dreams and those who LIVE their dreams.

Peer-to-Peer Accountability: The Most Effective Form

Patrick Lencioni, author of *The Ideal Team Player* and *The Five Dysfunctions of a Team*, argues that the best form of accountability is peer-to-peer. Peer pressure, when harnessed positively, can be more efficient and effective than top-down accountability. It fosters a culture of mutual responsibility where everyone is committed to collective success.

Don't LEAVE Your DREAM—LIVE It with Accountability!

Accountability is the backbone of success. It keeps us honest, driven, and focused on our goals. In your journey to live life big, embrace the accountability partnership factor. Find a PEER who will support you, challenge you, and walk alongside you as you turn your dreams into reality. Remember, you can't do life big alone—you need the right team with the same theme, and accountability partners who will ensure you never give up on your dreams.

Self-Activity for Chapter Ten

Reflect on these powerful questions to understand how accountability can bridge the gap between your intentions and actions. This self-activity will help you establish effective accountability partnerships to bring your dreams to life.

1. **Who Are Your Accountability Partners?**
   Identify the people who can hold you accountable for your goals. Are they positive, enriching, and encouraging? How can they support your journey?

2. **What Are You Accountable For?**
   Clarify your goals. What specific actions or milestones do you need accountability for, and how will you measure progress?

3. **How Often Will You Check In?**
   Accountability requires regular check-ins. How often will you meet or communicate with your accountability partner to review progress?

4. **What Obstacles Might Arise?**
   Anticipate challenges or excuses that could derail your efforts. How can your accountability partner help you stay focused and overcome these obstacles?

5. **What's Your Plan for Success?**
   Develop a clear, actionable plan with your accountability partner. How will you ensure that you remain consistent and committed to your dream?

These questions will guide you in building a solid accountability partnership to stay on track and turn your intentions into reality!

CHAPTER ELEVEN
MENTORSHIP FACTOR: ACCELERATING YOUR JOURNEY

The Power of a Mentor: A Catalyst for Transformation

"The hardest thing about leadership is finding the right people to follow you; the hardest thing about life is finding the right people to follow." — John Maxwell.

Mentorship is the hidden gem that can elevate your life from ordinary to extraordinary. Just as a catalyst speeds up a chemical reaction, a mentor accelerates your growth by offering wisdom, guidance, and support that would take years to acquire on your own. The right mentor sees your potential long before you do, challenging you to stretch beyond your limits and achieve what you once thought was impossible.

My Mentorship Story: Unlocking Potential Through Guided Wisdom

"He that is taught only by himself has a fool for a mentor." — Benjamin Jonson.

The Myth of Going Solo

For many years, I believed that personal growth was something you achieved on your own. Armed with ambition and access to information, I thought that my hard work alone would be enough to take me to new heights. I thought mentorship was a bonus, not a necessity.

However, I soon discovered the limitation of self-reliance. No matter how much determination I had, I found myself hitting ceilings I couldn't break through alone. My growth was stunted, not because of a lack of effort, but because I was only looking through the lens of my own experiences. It became clear that I needed mentors—people who had already walked the path I was attempting to navigate.

As Benjamin Jonson said, "He that is taught only by himself has a fool for a mentor." And this was true for me—mentorship became the missing key to unlock my potential.

The Game-Changer: Joining the Maxwell Leadership Team

My journey took a dramatic turn when I joined the Maxwell Leadership Team and began receiving mentorship from Dr. John Maxwell, one of the world's most respected leadership experts. Under his guidance, I realized just how powerful having a seasoned mentor could be.

Dr. John Maxwell didn't just teach me about leadership; he modeled it. He pushed me to go beyond what I thought was possible and gave me the tools and mindset to grow exponentially. His mentorship was a game-changer in my life, but it didn't stop there.

The Maxwell Leadership Team is filled with mentors whose influence has shaped my journey in remarkable ways. Valorie Burton was my go-to for coaching expertise, while Mark Cole sharpened my leadership development skills. Chris Robinson guided me on attitude and business building, and Roddy Galbraith was instrumental in honing my communication skills. Elizabeth McCormick empowered me in professional speaking, and Deb Ingino led me deeper into executive leadership through DISC training and the Executive Program.

A Global Influence: Mentors Beyond the Maxwell Team

In addition to the powerhouse mentors from the Maxwell Team, I've had the honor of being influenced by some of the greatest minds across various industries:

- Dr. Myles Munroe taught me about the power of purpose.

- Dr. David Oyedepo demonstrated the importance of faith-driven leadership.

- Ed Mylett inspired me to push beyond my comfort zone.

- Anthony Robbins taught me the principles of personal transformation.

- Craig Groeschel emphasized the importance of authenticity in leadership.

- Dr. Kenneth Copeland, Dr. Jerry Savelle, Dr. Jesse Duplantis, Dr. Mike Murdock, and Keith Moore played vital roles in shaping my spiritual and leadership journey.

These mentors didn't just offer advice; they imparted a lifetime of wisdom, broadened my horizons, and accelerated my growth. They gave me the push I needed to stop dreaming small and start taking massive action.

The Impact of Mentorship: A Catalyst for Transformation

"The delicate balance of mentoring someone is not creating them in your own image but giving them the opportunity to create themselves." — Steven Spielberg.

Mentorship does more than just guide you—it transforms you. Here's what mentorship has done for me:

- Expanded My Vision: My mentors saw potential in me that I didn't see in myself. They encouraged me to dream bigger and push boundaries I hadn't dared to before.

- Kept Me Accountable: Whether it was launching new projects or refining my leadership style, my mentors always held me accountable to my goals and helped me stay on track.

- Offered Real-World Experience: While theory is essential, nothing beats the insights gained from someone who has been where you want to go. My mentors shared real-world experiences, helping me avoid mistakes and fast-tracking my success.

- Provided Honest Feedback: Mentors provide the kind of feedback that doesn't flatter but fuels growth. Their insights gave me a clear view of where I needed to improve, and their encouragement kept me going when I doubted myself.

Why Mentorship Matters: The Difference Between Success and Struggle

"A mentor is someone who sees more talent and ability within you, than you see in yourself, and helps bring it out of you." – Bob Proctor.

Mentorship is not a luxury; it's a necessity for anyone serious about growth. It bridges the gap between where you are and where you want to be.

Here's why it matters:

- Faster Growth: You can spend years figuring things out on your own, or you can achieve results faster with someone guiding you.

- New Perspectives: Mentors help you see things you would have missed otherwise.

- Encouragement: On tough days, a mentor's encouragement is priceless.

- Skill Development: Mentorship exposes you to new skills, knowledge, and strategies that can propel you forward.

Mentorship: The Ultimate Accelerator

"Show me a successful individual and I'll show you someone who had real positive influences in his or her life. I don't care what you do for a living—if you do it well, I'm sure there was someone cheering you on or showing the way." — Denzel Washington.

Mentorship is the rocket fuel that accelerates your personal and professional growth. If you're serious about living your dream, you need to seek out mentors who have already traveled the path. They are the bridge between intention and success.

I've learned that no one can go far alone. Your dream may be uniquely yours, but the journey requires the support and wisdom of others. Surround yourself with mentors, and you'll find yourself achieving things you never thought possible.

Embrace Mentorship, Live Your Dream and Live Life Big!

"Mentorship is the key to unlocking the potential within." — Oprah Winfrey.

The mentors I've had in my life have given me the strength, knowledge, and courage to pursue my dreams with relentless passion. Without them, I would have settled for less than I was capable of. Now, I make it my mission to pay it forward by mentoring others and sharing the wisdom I've gained along the way.

As you embark on your journey, I encourage you to seek out mentors who can help you reach your highest potential. Don't try to go it alone—surround yourself with people who inspire, challenge, and support you. Your dream is worth it.

Mentorship: A Lifeline in the Sea of Challenges

"A mentor is someone who allows you to see the hope inside yourself." — Oprah Winfrey.

Life's journey is fraught with challenges—moments of doubt, setbacks, and fears that can leave you adrift. A mentor is like a lighthouse in these stormy seas, guiding you back to your path when the waves of life threaten to overwhelm you. My own experience under the mentorship of Dr. John Maxwell has been transformative. His mentorship has provided me with a clear vision, a sense of direction, and the tools to navigate the complexities of leadership and personal growth.

Why Mentorship Matters: The Ripple Effect

"The best way a mentor can prepare another leader is to expose him or her to other great people." — John Maxwell.

Mentorship is not just about personal growth; it's about creating a ripple effect. When you receive guidance, you're also empowered to pass it on, impacting others and contributing to a cycle of continuous improvement. The beauty of mentorship lies in its ability to multiply success—what you learn from your mentor, you can teach others, creating a legacy of wisdom and growth.

The MENTORSHIP Advantage: Unlocking Your Full Potential

Mentorship is an invaluable asset that can transform your life in myriad ways. Here's a deeper look into what mentorship stands for using the simple acronym, MENTORSHIP:

- **M = Motivation:** A mentor ignites your passion, pushing you to go further than you ever thought possible.

- **E = Expanded Perspectives:** Mentors broaden your worldview, helping you see opportunities and solutions you might have overlooked.

- **N = Networking Opportunities:** Mentors connect you with people who can help you achieve your goals, opening doors that would otherwise remain closed.

- **T = Transfer [Knowledge Transfer]:** A mentor imparts wisdom and knowledge, equipping you with the tools needed for success.

- **O = Observation Laboratory:** Through mentorship, you observe firsthand how success is achieved, providing you with a model to emulate.

- **R = Relationship:** A mentor offers a relationship based on trust, where you can grow in a safe and supportive environment.

- **S = Support and Guidance:** Mentors provide unwavering support, helping you navigate challenges and celebrate victories.

- **H = Honest Feedback:** A mentor gives you honest, constructive feedback, helping you refine your approach and improve continuously.

- **I = Inspiration:** A mentor inspires you to dream bigger, think broader, and act with greater purpose.

- **P = Personal and Professional Growth:** Mentorship accelerates both personal and professional growth, helping you achieve your full potential.

Metaphors and Inspiring Quotes on Mentors

- **Mentors: The Architects of Destiny**

    "A mentor empowers a person to see a possible future and believe it can be obtained." — Shawn Hitchcock.

- **The Mentor's Map: Charting the Course to Success**

"Show me a successful individual, and I'll show you someone who had real positive influences in his or her life. I don't care what you do for a living—if you do it well, I'm sure there was someone cheering you on or showing the way. A mentor." — Denzel Washington.

- **The Ripple Effect of Mentorship: Creating Legacies**

"Our chief want in life is somebody who will make us do what we can." — Ralph Waldo Emerson.

- **From Potential to Performance: The Mentor's Role**

"One of the greatest values of mentors is the ability to see ahead what others cannot see and to help them navigate a course to their destination." — John Maxwell.

Embrace Your DREAM with Mentorship Factor

Mentorship is not just a factor in achieving your dreams—it's a force multiplier that can turn those dreams into reality. By embracing mentorship, you're not only investing in your future but also contributing to a legacy that can inspire others to do the same.

Eleanor Roosevelt, a former first lady of the United States said, "The future belongs to those who believe in the beauty of their dreams." With the guidance of a mentor, your dream, fortified by resilience, teamwork, accountability, and mentorship, can indeed shape a brighter future for yourself and others.

Self-Activity for Chapter Eleven

"The best effect of any book is that it excites the reader to self-activity." – Thomas Carlyle.

Reflect on these powerful questions to explore how mentorship can accelerate your journey and unlock your potential. Use them to identify the right mentors and maximize the impact of their guidance on your dreams.

1. **Who Are Your Mentors?**
   Identify the mentors in your life. Who are the people you look up to for guidance and wisdom? How have they shaped your journey so far?

2. **What Skills or Knowledge Do You Need?**
   Consider the areas in which you want to grow. What specific skills or knowledge would a mentor help you develop? Who could provide that expertise?

3. **How Can You Be More Intentional in Seeking Mentorship?**
   Mentorship doesn't happen by accident. How can you actively seek out mentors who align with your goals and values? What steps will you take to connect with them?

4. **How Will You Apply What You Learn?**
   Mentors provide wisdom, but it's up to you to apply it. How will you take action on the insights and advice they give you?

5. **How Can You Pay It Forward?**
   Mentorship is a cycle. How can you use what you've learned to mentor others and help them along their journey?

These questions will help you embrace mentorship as a powerful tool for personal and professional growth, accelerating your journey toward your dreams!

EPILOGUE
LIVE LIFE BIG—YOUR DREAM AWAITS YOU!

"Dying is nothing. What is terrible is not to live." – Victor Hugo.

Writing this book has been a deeply fulfilling journey, not just because of the content, but because this is how I live—not merely theories from another book. It is my personal experience. Legendary basketball coach John Wooden once said: "The most powerful leadership tool you have is your personal example." That message still ignites hearts today.

One of the greatest lessons I've learned from my mentor, Dr. John Maxwell, is the Law of Credibility: *"Your most effective message is the one you live."* I've seen a tremendous transformation in my life, personally and professionally, as I began focusing on living what I learned. This book is not the work of a philosopher—it is a lived-out experience.

LIVE YOUR DREAM—Not Someone Else's!

Living life big is not reserved for a select few. It's for anyone willing to make the sacrifice. But remember, sacrifice is not a one-time act; it's an ongoing commitment. If you don't sacrifice for what you want, what you want becomes the sacrifice.

Sixteen years ago, I immigrated to the United States. I chose not to live the life others expected of me, remaining a physician. Instead, I embraced the courage to live life on my terms—living my dream. Eleanor Brownn said it best: "You only have one life to live. Make sure it's yours."

Which Life Are You Living?

There are three types of people in the world:
1. Those who merely exist, making no meaningful contribution.
2. Those who live life small, far below their potential.
3. Those rare, the few who dare to LIVE LIFE BIG.

Simon Sinek, a thought leader and optimist, wisely noted: "The true cost of following your dreams isn't what you sacrifice when you chase them, it's what you lose when you don't." The real price of not living your dream is the missed opportunity to make a difference in countless lives across the world.

Designing Your Dream Life

Coach John Wooden, a beacon of wisdom, said: "If you want to live your dream, focus on what you can do—not on what others, fate, or luck must do for you." Success is not luck; it's design. Marissa Nehlsen, a dear friend, fellow Maxwell Leadership Team Certified Speaker and CEO of a 7-figure financial firm, said: "A dream life doesn't just drop into your lap. A dream life is something that has to be designed."

Two of my great mentors, to whom this book is dedicated—Dr. Myles Munroe and Dr. David Oyedepo—modelled this principle. Dr. David Oyedepo still lives these principles even as he approaches his seventy years on planet earth. Raised dirt poor, they both designed their dream lives and lived them big. They were not born into wealth, but they both designed their lives and LIVED LIFE BIG. This book is dedicated to these two giants.

Dr. Myles Munroe—The Visionary Extraordinaire Who Lived a Life of Purpose!

Dr. Myles Munroe once said, "The greatest tragedy in life is not death, but life without a purpose." Despite growing up poor in the Bahamas, he went on to touch millions of lives through his teachings on leadership and purpose. Even ten years after his passing, his legacy continues to inspire. He was a man of vision, a teacher of teachers, and a true example of living life big.

Dr. Myles Munroe was a leader of leaders, a philosopher, and a transformational mentor.

Dr. David Oyedepo—The Architect of Impact!

Dr. David Oyedepo, a mentor of mentors, once said, "Success is not in position or accumulation, but in making tangible contributions to your generation." As the founder of one of the largest churches in the world, his life is a testament to **living life big**. He taught me that life is not about what you take but about what you give. This mindset has shaped my life and work.

Dr. David Oyedepo, founder of Living Faith Church Worldwide, epitomizes what it means to live life big. His work has transformed and is still transforming countless lives all around the world with visible impact. As he turns 70 in a few weeks, his life stands as a living testament that living life big is not the exclusive preserve of some people—it's for all who dare to live their dreams.

The Faith Tabernacle in Nigeria, under the leadership of Bishop David Oyedepo, made global headlines in 1999 when it was recognized by the Guinness Book of Records as one of the largest church buildings in the world, with an awe-inspiring seating capacity of 50,000 people. Now, the Living Faith Church Worldwide, also known as Winners Chapel, is once again set to make history with The Ark

Project. This monumental facility, which will serve as the new International Headquarters, is slated for dedication on November 29, 2025, in Ota, Ogun State, Nigeria. With a seating capacity of over 200,000, it will stand as a beacon of faith and vision, showcasing the limitless potential of human ambition when fueled by purpose and divine inspiration.

These remarkable achievements are not simply extraordinary feats—they symbolize something far greater. They serve as living proof that "living life big" is not the exclusive right of a select few, but an attainable reality for anyone who dares to dream, believe, and take the necessary steps. The Ark Project is a towering testament to the fact that when you align your vision with unwavering faith and relentless action, the impossible becomes possible. Everyone has the potential to achieve greatness and live life on a grand scale, provided they are willing to embrace the mindset, discipline, and tenacity required to turn their dreams into reality.

Who's to Blame If You Don't Live Life Big?

Viktor Frankl, a Holocaust survivor and philosopher, once said, "Life is never made unbearable by circumstances, but only by lack of meaning and purpose." If you don't live life big, who will you blame? Your circumstances? Those who have faced worse have still risen to live their dreams.

Hard work is the cure for a hard life. Publilius Syrus, a Latin writer, said, "It's a bad thing to become accustomed to good luck." Don't wait for luck. Wake up and live your dream.

Dare to Live Life Big!

Every morning presents you with a pivotal choice: you can either stay asleep and let your dreams fade or rise with purpose and chase them relentlessly. As one wise man once said, "Sacrifice a little sleep, because poverty is born in the bed. You can't sleep like you're in a race with the dead and expect to thrive in the land of the living."

Living Life Big is not about comfort but getting out of your comfort zone—it's about embracing hard work, making sacrifices, and being relentless in the pursuit of your vision. Your dream wasn't given to you by chance—it was placed in your heart for a reason, and it's calling you to step up, stretch beyond your limits, and take bold action.

This is your moment.

Success doesn't wait for the idle. It's time to rise, defy the odds, and go after the life you were destined to live. Don't just dream—live your dream with passion, courage, and unshakable determination. The world is waiting for what only you can offer.

Dare to Live Life Big! Your future is in your hands—make it count!!!!

Final Charge: Go and LIVE LIFE BIG!

I believe in you! Now that you have the **blueprint**, there is no reason for you to ever leave your dream behind again. Instead, I challenge you to *live* your dream with unwavering commitment, passion, and relentless pursuit of greatness. You were created to live a life of significance, a life that is *BIG* and full of purpose!

As **Walt Disney** said, *"All our dreams can come true, if we have the courage to pursue them."* So, go forward with boldness and courage. The road may not always be easy, but the dream is worth every step you take. You have the tools, the vision, and the ability to **LIVE LIFE BIG**—now it's time to act!

"Don't ask yourself what the world needs; ask yourself what makes you come alive. And then go do that. Because what the world needs is people who have come alive." – Howard Thurman.

I encourage you to dream big, live fearlessly, and never settle for less than what you were meant to be. Your dream is not just about you—it's about the impact you can have on others, the difference you can make in the world. **LIVE YOUR DREAM, because someone out there needs the greatness that only you can bring!**

I would love to hear how this book has inspired and impacted your life. **Email me** at *wordsmith626@gmail.com* and share your story—I'm excited to celebrate your journey with you!

With belief in your potential and dreams,

Your friend,
Dr. Michael Koku
+1-484-466-1036

Go and LIVE LIFE BIG! Because you were made for more!

MEET THE AUTHOR

Dr. Michael Koku is a Physician, and Maxwell Leadership Team Independent Executive Director, Speaker, Coach, and Trainer. He has a unique ability to simplify complex ideas and deliver them in a compelling, actionable way. With a mission to empower leaders both personally and professionally, Dr. Koku has ignited transformation for professionals across the globe virtually and in person on demand via his leadership development, personal growth training, executive coaching and global leadership conferences that he hosts via the LAMP Global Community in collaboration with twenty-one dynamic leaders.

His dynamic coaching, leadership training, and keynote speaking have inspired excellence in different streams of influence like business, education, healthcare, government and religion. As the author of ten influential books, including *4 Keys for Effective Leadership*, *Understanding Your Gift 2.0*, *The AREA Code: Unveiling the Essence of Servant Leadership*, and *LIVE LIFE BIG: Don't LEAVE Your DREAM, LIVE Your DREAM*, Dr. Koku continues to shape the modern leadership landscape. His works offer practical strategies for navigating the challenges of today's complex world.

Leading the LAMP Global Community, Dr. Koku drives initiatives like WILL [Women In Leadership League], PEARL [Parents Empowered Academy for Right Leadership], YES [Youth Empowerment Society], and TBN [The Berean Network], which empower leaders across eight areas of influence: Government, Sports, Business, Family, Religion, Arts and Entertainment, Media, and Education. His unwavering passion for making a meaningful difference resonates through every endeavor, whether he's facilitating leadership development sessions, coaching leaders one-on-one, or delivering powerful keynote addresses.

What sets Dr. Koku apart is his commitment to measurable outcomes and tangible success. His passion for serving others drives his belief that true fulfillment comes from lifting others and leaving a positive mark on the world. Through his impactful work, he continually empowers individuals to unlock their full potential and create lasting, meaningful change.

ESPERANZA MANIFOLD CONCEPTS LLC

Esperanza Manifold Concepts LLC is your gateway to exceptional leadership, personal growth, and executive coaching. Under the seasoned guidance of Dr. Michael Koku, a Maxwell Leadership Team Executive Director, Speaker, Coach, and Trainer, we empower individuals and organizations to elevate their potential through world-class, customized training and development sessions. Whether you're looking to develop leaders, strengthen teams, or enhance human capital, Esperanza Manifold Concepts LLC delivers transformational results designed to meet your unique needs.

Our extensive reach spans the globe, having trained professionals in the United States, Canada, the United Kingdom, Italy, Saudi Arabia, Nigeria, Burkina Faso, Botswana, Kenya, Ghana, the Netherlands, and India. Through both in-person and virtual platforms like Zoom and Microsoft Teams, we've made a lasting impact in sectors like Education, Business, Government, Healthcare, and Nonprofit organizations. The outcomes speak for themselves: powerful transformation, enhanced team dynamics, and a renewed energy to achieve organizational goals.

At Esperanza Manifold Concepts LLC, we don't just train—we inspire you and your team to reach your fullest potential, live your dreams, and embrace the opportunity to *live life big*. As John C. Maxwell says, "Leadership is not about titles, positions, or flowcharts. It is about one life influencing another." Let us be the catalyst that inspires and influences your team to greatness.

Contact us today at 484-466-1036 or visit lgcleadership.com/esperanza to unlock the potential within your organization!

LAMP GLOBAL COMMUNITY

Unlocking Infinite Growth, Empowering Leaders, Transforming Futures Globally.

At **LAMP Global Community**, we believe that leadership is not a solitary journey, but a shared path of growth, empowerment, and transformation. Our mission is to **attract, develop, and multiply leaders** who are committed to unlocking their infinite growth potential and equipping others to lead with excellence. Together, we are shaping a future where leadership is intentional, impactful, and inclusive.

In just 19 months, what began as a dream has flourished into a thriving global network of **21 dedicated leaders**, united by shared values and a positive attitude. Our community is driven by a clear purpose: to **collaborate, empower, and transform lives** through leadership, education, and service. We bring this to life through our quarterly global projects, initiatives, and conferences, creating lasting change across continents.

Our Key Pillars:

- **Collaboration**: We build leaders together, working
- **Empowerment**: We equip emerging leaders with the tools, mindset, and support they need to thrive.
- **Global Transformation**: Through our leadership programs and initiatives, we are committed to creating a ripple effect of positive change worldwide.

As the parent organization for **WILL** (Women In Leadership League), **PEARL** (Parents Empowered Academy for Right Leadership), **YES** (Youth

Empowerment Society), and **TBN** (The Berean Network), LAMP Global Community is at the forefront of shaping leaders in every sphere of influence. Our reach is wide, but our focus is clear: **to create a unified, empowered global leadership movement.**

Our Collective Accomplishments:

- Leadership Masterclasses that have equipped individuals to realize their leadership potential.

- Hosting **five virtual global conferences** that have transformed the lives of men, women, parents, and youth from around the world.

- Preparing for the upcoming **MADE FOR MORE GLOBAL LEADERSHIP CONFERENCE 4.0** in March 2025, focusing on servant leadership and its impact on communities and organizations.

The Power of TEAM:

"Together Everyone Achieves More" is more than just an acronym—it's the heartbeat of our community. We believe in the synergy of collective effort and the undeniable truth that **teamwork makes the dream work**. With every step forward, we prove that when individuals unite around a shared vision, we can achieve far more than we could alone.

Join Us: Be part of a global movement dedicated to **unlocking leadership potential, empowering lives, and transforming futures**. Together, we will not only realize our dreams but amplify them into something truly extraordinary. **LAMP Global Community** invites you to be a beacon of leadership, sparking change and guiding others toward greatness.

"Talent wins games, but teamwork and intelligence win championships." — *Michael Jordan.*

Let's **build the future of leadership—together!**

Website: lgcleadership.com

Book Summary

LIVE LIFE BIG: Don't LEAVE Your Dream, LIVE Your Dream!

In *LIVE LIFE BIG: Don't LEAVE Your Dream, LIVE Your Dream!* You are invited by the author, Dr. Michael Koku, on a life-changing journey to stop settling for less and start living the life you were meant to live. Too many people abandon their dreams, trapped by fear, doubt, and the expectations of others. This book is your wake-up call—a bold declaration that **living life big** is not reserved for the privileged few. It is possible for anyone willing to take the leap.

With compelling stories, practical advice, and inspirational quotes from some of the greatest leaders and thinkers of our time, this book shows you how to ignite your passion, overcome obstacles, and stay relentless in the pursuit of your dream. From understanding the true cost of not following your dream to designing a life that reflects your deepest desires, *LIVE LIFE BIG* offers you the tools and mindset to transform your life.

Drawing from the lived experiences of the author and insights from world-renowned mentors like Coach John Wooden, Dr. John Maxwell, Dr. Myles Munroe, and Dr. David Oyedepo, you'll learn that success is not about luck but about taking action, embracing sacrifice, and living with purpose. The book challenges you to stop making excuses and start living boldly, because your dream is not just about you—it's about the countless lives you will impact.

If you've ever felt like you're capable of more or that your dreams are slipping away, *LIVE LIFE BIG* will inspire you to **wake up, chase your dream, and live a life of significance**. The world needs your dream—don't leave it, **live it!**

Made in the USA
Middletown, DE
29 September 2024